# MAKING THE MOST OF COLLEGE

This book has been awarded Harvard University Press's annual prize for an outstanding publication about education and society, established in 1995 by the Virginia and Warren Stone Fund.

RICHARD J. LIGHT

# MAKING THE
# MOST OF COLLEGE

STUDENTS

SPEAK

THEIR

MINDS

HARVARD
UNIVERSITY
PRESS
Cambridge,
Massachusetts
London,
England

*Library of Congress Cataloging-in-Publication Data*
Light, Richard J.
Making the most of college: students speak their minds/Richard J.
Light.
    p. cm.
Includes bibliographical references (p. ) and index.
ISBN 0-674-00478-7 (alk. paper)
    1. Harvard University–Students–Attitudes–Longitudinal studies.
2. College seniors–Attitudes–Longitudinal studies.  I. Title.
LD2160.L54 2001
378.1'98—dc21       00-059728

Fifth printing, 2001

I dedicate this book to my family. To Pat, who shares my life. To Jen and Sarah, who know they are the whole point of the enterprise. To my mother, Mura Light Stifel, who has given me a lifetime of love, and even suggested a title for this book. To Max, a kind, fun-loving stepfather. And most of all, to the memory of my father.

# CONTENTS

# MAKING THE MOST OF COLLEGE

# 1

## INTRODUCTION

Why do some undergraduates feel they are making the most of their years at college, while others are far less positive? What choices and attitudes distinguish between these two groups? What can an individual student do, and what can any college do, to improve the chances that on graduation day that student will say, "I really got what I came here for"?

I have been a professor for thirty years. Each year I meet with a new group of young advisees. And each year I think about these questions anew. What can I tell these young people at the outset that will help them make the most of their time in college?

Simultaneously, I wonder what thoughts I can share with my faculty colleagues. Anyone who teaches for any length of time gets caught up in a debate about how to help students learn as effectively as possible. My colleagues and I think long and hard about the best ways to advise students, to teach classes, and even to teach outside the classroom. Many think about how to enhance the quality of student life, especially on a modern campus that is increasingly racially and ethnically diverse. Doing these many aspects of our job well is not easy. Translating good intentions into practice poses a continuing challenge.

Some years ago I attended a gathering of faculty and senior administrators from more than fifty colleges and universities. Each was invited to present a view from his or her campus. What were the responsibilities of faculty, deans, and advisors for shaping students' overall experience at college? Not just in-class teaching, but the entire experience.

The first person to speak was a senior dean from a distinguished university. He announced proudly that he and his colleagues admit good students and then make a special effort to "get out of their way." "Students learn mostly from one another," he argued. "We shouldn't muck up that process."

I was dismayed. Soon my own daughters would begin thinking about where to go to college. What I had just heard was the exact opposite of what I hoped would await them. I had come to the meeting hoping to learn how other colleges and universities were working to help their undergraduates succeed. I expected to hear how campus leaders were trying to improve teaching and advising and the overall quality of student life. I wanted to know how each institution was helping students to do their jobs better. Instead, I was hearing a senior official from a major university describe an astonishing strategy: find good students and then neglect them.

I have never forgotten that remark. It got me to think hard about what decisions new students, as well as administrators and faculty members, can make to facilitate the best possible undergraduate experience. Since that meeting I have participated in ten years of systematic research to explore that question. I believe we have some promising answers. And after visiting more than ninety other colleges and universities, sharing key ideas, I am convinced that these answers apply to most campuses across America, including many that are very different from my own.

In this book I offer a synthesis of findings from years of research on two broad questions. First, what choices can students themselves make to get the most out of college? Second, what are effective ways for faculty members and campus leaders to translate good intentions into practice?

For several years, more than sixty faculty members from more than twenty colleges and universities met regularly to design ways to answer such questions. Both faculty and students have been pursuing these inquiries. Many of the projects are now complete. Strong findings are emerging and are beginning to influence teaching, learning, advising, and residential life at Harvard and at some other colleges. In this book I want to tell you what we've found out.

## Plan of the Book

Each chapter that follows focuses on certain choices a student must make at college. I have learned from interviewing students that some make these choices carefully and purposefully, while others make them haphazardly, with little thought and planning. The consequences often are profound. Many students say, on graduation day, "I wouldn't have done it any other way. It was a great experience." Yet a significant minority lament, "If only I had known."

A key theme in students' interviews is the strong interplay of different features of campus life. Course choices, advising, and decisions about residential life do not stand in isolation. They are part of a connected system. For example, the educational impact of racial and ethnic diversity on today's campuses is closely tied to choices students make about whom to live with and spend time with. In Chapter 2 I make the case for integrating these different parts of campus life. The chapter offers an organizing principle for thinking about one's college years in ways that can increase their meaning.

In Chapter 3 I present a series of specific suggestions

from students to their fellow students about how to deal with predictable questions. How can I get off to a good start? Will part-time work to earn money affect my schoolwork? What is a good way to find help if I need it? How should I think about choosing a place to live?

Chapter 4 focuses on what makes certain classes especially memorable for students. Hint: it is not primarily how much the professor knows—or how big or small the class is—or even whether it meets after 10 o'clock in the morning.

Chapter 5 describes especially helpful advising. Students point out repeatedly that getting constructive, somewhat personalized advice may be the single most underestimated feature of a great college experience.

Chapter 6 summarizes students' descriptions of how certain faculty members make a special difference in their lives. The punch line is that faculty members count more than they often realize. I hope students at all colleges will consider how they might find professors who will have a positive and powerful impact on them.

Chapters 7 and 8 explore the impact of dramatic demographic changes on campus. This new diversity has inspired delight, fear, conflict, new opportunities, and endless conferences. These chapters present students' perspectives on how the new racial and ethnic diversity affects learning, both inside and outside of classrooms.

One point that emerges from these two chapters is that broad generalizations about the educational effects of students from different backgrounds studying, working, and playing together are often wrong and rarely helpful. Racial and ethnic diversity can, and often does, enhance learning in the classroom and beyond. The examples students give tend to be far more positive than negative. Yet few students from any background have the slightest trouble illustrating how, for them personally, this same diversity has at specific times had negative effects.

This mix of stories carries policy suggestions for students as individuals, and especially for campus leaders. It becomes clear in these chapters that details of campus policies matter a lot. The leadership at colleges, including student leaders, can do much to create a positive atmosphere—an atmosphere in which the benefits of diversity are maximized and unproductive conflicts are minimized.

Each student has a story to tell. Taken together, their stories reveal certain common themes. For example, many students of all racial and ethnic backgrounds draw a sharp contrast between positive experiences they are having with diversity at college and negative experiences they had in high school. Many undergraduates believe they understand exactly why their experiences in the two settings are so different, and their reasons sound both judicious and compelling. These differences lead them to offer suggestions both to fellow students and to those who run colleges. Many of their suggestions emphasize the critical role of residential living arrangements because of the remarkable amount of learning that occurs in residential interactions.

Chapter 9 offers specific suggestions from students to campus leaders. It is striking how many students seek leadership from administrators, deans, residence hall directors, and even college presidents. Most students don't really want us to just admit them and "get out of their way." And since nearly all students experience both fulfilling and frustrating occurrences in their years at college, they understandably want the people in charge working systematically to maximize the former and minimize the latter. Several of their suggestions would be easy to implement. One or two others would require a certain degree of courage.

## Learning from Students

I am a statistician, but I am impressed by the power of individuals' heartfelt stories. Throughout this book, I use quotations from students' interviews to illustrate each point. Students who agreed to be interviewed were told that they might be quoted. Several actively urged me to include specific stories they thought would be helpful to future students. Many of those stories are here. I have edited the quotations a bit, omitting "ums" and "ahs," reducing repetition, and, with each student's permission, occasionally tightening the prose to make a point clear.

Where did all these stories come from? All findings in this book come from in-depth interviews. Early on, my colleagues and I decided that to learn what works best for students, we should ask them. So we did. More than sixteen hundred undergraduates have been interviewed during this effort, many of them more than once. Some were interviewed by faculty members: I myself interviewed four hundred. Other interviews were conducted by undergraduates, who were carefully trained and supervised by faculty members. Interviews ranged from one to three hours.

These personal interviews paint an entirely different picture from the kind of information that comes from a large-scale, check-box style of survey questionnaire. As a statistician, I know there are many circumstances in which questionnaires with check-box categories are a superb format for gathering evidence. In fact, I teach a course on this topic. Yet for this particular research, personal interviews offer a special depth and richness that no check-box questionnaire, however well designed, could easily tap.

One reason is that the personal interviews are loaded with details. It is one thing for a student to say that a particular class had a powerful impact on her thinking. It is far more useful to understand *why* this class had such power, how it was organized, and whether other faculty members and students can benefit in their own work from this success story. The more illustrations a student can offer to buttress a point, the better and more helpful that point is for other students.

For me, interviewing four hundred undergraduates was a special pleasure. Harvard undergraduates have strong views. They come here expecting a lot. Nearly all are enthusiastic and productive, and nearly all quickly become overcommitted. The best part is, nearly all students also have suggestions for improving both academic and nonacademic aspects of college. They constantly question what we do, what they do, how to do it better, what they are getting and giving in this demanding community. Their convictions are changing the way I, and many of my colleagues, think about teaching and advising.

## Findings and Surprises

I hope students reading this book will find many of the results useful. Advice from fellow undergraduates, based on their own experiences both good and bad, should be helpful as students think about making decisions. What to look for when choosing classes, and the faculty members who teach them? How to interact most productively with advisors and mentors? What to consider when deciding about living arrangements? How to allocate time? The students we interviewed have suggestions about all these topics.

Some of what we have learned from students fits what we expected, but certain insights are surprising, at least to me. Let me preview nine of our findings here. And these are just the beginning.

First, I assumed that most important and memorable academic learning goes on inside the classroom, while outside activities provide a useful but modest supplement. The evidence shows that the opposite is true: learning outside of classes, especially in residential settings and extracurricular activities such as the arts, is vital. When we asked students to think of a specific, critical incident or moment that had changed them profoundly, four-fifths of them chose a situation or event outside of the classroom.

Second, I expected students to prefer courses in which they could work at their own pace, courses with relatively few quizzes, exams, and papers until the end of the term. Wrong again. A large majority of students say they learn significantly more in courses that are highly structured, with relatively many quizzes and short assignments. Crucial to this preference is getting quick feedback from the professor— ideally with an opportunity to revise and make changes before receiving a final grade. In contrast, students are frustrated and disappointed with classes that require only a final paper. How can we ever improve our work, they ask, when the only feedback comes after a course is over, and when no revision is invited?

A third surprise has to do with homework. When I was in college years ago, nearly every professor announced that I should do my homework alone. Discussing problem sets or essay assignments with other students, I was told, would be considered cheating. Yet at many campuses today, professors increasingly are encouraging students to work together on homework assignments. Some faculty members are even creating small study groups in their courses, to help students work together outside of class.

A few students tell of professors who give homework assignments that are so challenging or complex that the only way to get the work done is to collaborate. To complete such assignments, students have to work cooperatively, dividing up the readings and meeting outside of class to teach one another. Many undergraduates report that such homework assignments increase both their learning and their engagement with a class. This alteration in the format of homework is a genuine cultural change, one that is happening on campuses across the country.

A fourth finding: student after student brings up the importance of class size in his or her academic development. Not surprisingly, small-group tutorials, small seminars, and one-to-one supervision are, for many, their capstone experience. Yet what I find surprising is that some undergraduates, when asked to identify a particularly critical or profound experience at college, identify a mentored internship *not done for academic credit.* The word "mentor" is used in many ways, and undergraduates we interviewed are very clear about what constitutes effective mentoring. A key idea here is that students get to create their own project and then implement it under the supervision of a faculty member. Instead of following a professor's plan, they face the new challenge of developing their own plan and applying it to a topic they care about.

Fifth, for most students the impact of racial and ethnic diversity on their college experience is strong. An overwhelming majority of undergraduates characterize its effects as highly positive. Students can learn much from others who come from different backgrounds, whether ethnic, geographic, political, religious, or economic. Yet many point out that learning from people of different backgrounds does not always happen naturally. Campus atmosphere and especially residential living arrangements are crucial.

Ironically, even the happiest students are sharply critical of platitudes about the virtues of diversity. Most have experienced unpleasant moments, awkward encounters, and sometimes worse. They point out that only when certain preconditions are met does "the good stuff" actually happen. They also note the good news—that those preconditions are factors that campus leaders can do something about. Campus leaders can do much to shape an environment in which diversity strengthens learning.

A sixth finding: students who get the most out of college, who grow the most academically, and who are happiest organize their time to include activities with faculty members, or with several other students, focused around accomplishing substantive academic work. For some students this is difficult. Interacting in depth with faculty members or even with fellow students around substantive work does not always come naturally. Yet most students at Harvard learn to do it with great success. Both advisors and other faculty members can help this process along.

A seventh finding: I was surprised by students' strong attitude toward writing. I would have guessed that they value good writing, but I didn't realize how deeply many of them care about it, or how strongly they hunger for specific suggestions about how to improve it.

Eighth, I would have expected a general feeling among students that good advising is important. Yet that is a platitude. It is the specifics that are striking. A large majority of undergraduates describe particular activities outside the classroom as profoundly affecting their academic performance. Some point to study techniques, such as working in small groups outside of class. Others tell of more personal exercises, such as formal time-logging.

Ninth, I expected many undergraduates to characterize work in foreign languages and literatures as merely a requirement to be gotten out of the way. In fact, hardly any do this. Students talk about language courses with special enthusiasm. Many rate them among the best of all their classes. Alumni agree, and strongly. When asked why, both groups point to the way these courses are organized and taught.

There is a clear lesson here. Students have thought a lot about what works well for them. We can learn much from their insights. Often their insights are far more helpful, and more subtle, than any vague conventional wisdom about what constitutes a valuable college education.

## Do These Findings Generalize?

This is not just a Harvard story. My visits to other campuses have convinced me that the findings in this book apply broadly. At every college I visit, whether highly selective or not, private or public, large or small, national or regional, students are eager to share their experiences, to tell what works at their place. I am struck by how much of what students on other campuses say is similar to what Harvard students say.

Wherever I go, I ask faculty, students, and administrators whether the ideas and suggestions I present about teaching, advising, maximizing students' engagement, and capitalizing on diversity apply on their campus. On more than ninety campuses the response has been clear: "Yes, most of those ideas would work well here."

For example, I recently shared some findings from this book at a large public university on the West Coast. When I described the positive student reaction to meeting in small groups outside of classes to go over homework, readings, and problem sets, the reaction from both faculty and students was, "If it works at Harvard, it should be even more valuable here, where faculty resources are less plentiful." Enough other campuses have now implemented enough of the suggestions in this book that I believe it would be a shame to say, "Those findings are so Harvard." Maybe a select few won't generalize—for example, our findings about the importance of undergraduate residence halls apply only to residential colleges—but it is clear that most generalize quite well.

I know that enormous differences exist among American colleges. Yet at nearly all of them, administrators and faculty members share with students a wish to enhance learning, improve instruction, and organize their campuses so that racial and ethnic differences can make a positive contribution to everyone's experience. If the findings I present here help students and leaders on many campuses take a few steps toward achieving these outcomes, I will consider this book a great success.

# 2

## POWERFUL CONNECTIONS

When it comes to activities other than the courses they take, students are on their own. Especially on a residential campus, many tend to be active, driven, and heavily engaged with outside-of-class activities, including work to earn money many need. Few have the slightest problem finding one or two or three engagements in addition to their classes. Whether it is public service, the arts, music, athletics, a student-run newspaper or magazine, special interest groups, or religious organizations, an overwhelming majority of undergraduates are up to their ears in activities outside of class.

How do undergraduates view these extracurricular opportunities? As a chance to have fun. As a chance to learn new skills. As a chance to give something back to a community, or even a country, that has been good to them. As a chance to perform or direct or produce. As a chance to learn leadership skills. Even at a college as academically focused and intense as Harvard, most graduates have far clearer memories of their singing, or writing, or volunteer tutoring of recent immigrants, than of the details of the class on American history they took in sophomore year.

A week has 168 hours. A full-time student on most campuses, taking four courses during an academic term, spends between twelve and eighteen hours sitting in actual classrooms, taking classes. Those who major in humanities and social sciences tend to spend about twelve. Those majoring in a physical science spend some extra hours each week in labs, which can easily bring the total to about eighteen. So the bulk of students' lives is spent outside of the classroom.

That leads to a simple but enormously powerful finding that shines through interview after interview with graduating seniors. Those students who make connections between what goes on inside and outside the classroom report a more satisfying college experience. The students who find some way to connect their interest in music, for example, either with coursework or with an extracurricular volunteer activity or both, report a qualitatively different overall experience.

Do all students succeed in doing this? Of course not. Does it come automatically, or easily, even to those who end up doing it? Sometimes. But many don't think of it at first. Sometimes they figure it out because they are exceptionally thoughtful. Sometimes it happens because they stumble into it thanks to good fortune. But now, more and more often, advisors (including me) consciously encourage students to do this. We tell first-year students that their fellow undergraduates report that making connections between what they do inside and outside of classes can have a profound and positive impact on their precious years at college.

Incoming students seem to be taking this advice extraordinarily seriously. Perhaps this illustrates the power of gathering data directly from students. Telling newcomers on campus that people just three and four years older have something to suggest catches their attention quickly.

Perhaps the idea of making connections between in-class and out-of-class activities sounds obvious. Yet without some concrete illustrations of how to do it, and why it can be so helpful, the suggestion risks becoming an abstraction. Let's consider a few examples.

## Shall I Go to Med School?

On any campus, some students arrive thinking that after college they will go to medical school. During their four years as undergraduates, they try to figure out whether medical school is the right choice for them, or whether it really isn't what they want.

We ought to be able to advise such students constructively. Good advising can have a profound impact. A senior from Chicago got great help from the Office of Career Services. She sought advice on outside-of-classroom experiences that would help clarify her thinking about a future career in medicine. A counselor worked with her to arrange a summer internship at a large hospital in Chicago.

Working for little more than minimum wage, this twenty-year-old was asked by the hospital to get two programs up and running so they would continue after she returned to college in the fall. The first program changed the penalty for teenage smokers who incur minor legal infractions. In the past, they had generally been given a penalty of simple probation. Little or no learning took place. Their legal infractions resulted in little consequence either to themselves or to their communities.

The student created and implemented a new program. Rather than just receiving probation, each young offender was now required to perform a specific community service: the teenaged smokers were required to help older people in the community who were dying from smoking-related emphysema. Their tasks included shopping and carrying groceries.

The second program the student initiated was aimed at people of any age who were having a difficult time managing their own health, yet who were at high risk for coronary disease. This program arranged for each person to witness actual heart surgery, and then to talk with the heart patients afterward.

The student says that this summer experience profoundly changed the way she thought about all her academic work at college. In fact, it changed her entire future. She had planned to concentrate in biology with an eye toward medical school. Now, with great enthusiasm, she shifted her focus toward public policy, public health, and an environmental science major. The activities outside of class, and their connection to her academic work, gave her new insight about the real world, about what she was good at, and about what mattered to her. The summer at the hospital gave her a new purpose, and perspective, to design and plan her academic coursework.

## Political Science or Law School?

A young man majoring in government or political science gives a second example. He took the usual introductory courses, but he was uncertain about how it all fit together, at least for him. He was pretty sure by the end of his first year that he wanted, in the future, to be a professor. After all, he was getting a lot of A's. Always had. And he was comfortable with this plan, yet he felt one, troubling caveat: he had never really considered anything else.

So he decided to work with an inner-city self-help group in Boston, to improve the dilapidated and poorly maintained housing where they lived. The group had been started by several women who were welfare recipients and all lived in the same housing project, where the local housing authority was unable or unwilling to provide even the most basic maintenance services. Garbage piled up around their buildings, and the hallways reeked of urine. Throughout his sophomore year this young man worked with the group to develop a plan to improve their living conditions. He spent hundreds of hours lining up craftsmen of various sorts, with building skills, who were willing to volunteer their time and their labor.

The plan was for this painstakingly assembled group of volunteers to spend a spring weekend improving and refurbishing government-funded housing and working on inner-city infrastructure projects. But the plan was stopped cold. A large trade union in Boston went to court and got an injunction to stop this young man's volunteer brigade. The union cited, according to this student, laws that make it illegal for craftsmen to volunteer their labor for any part of government-funded projects to improve housing for poor people. The trade union lawyer also cited the Fair Labor Standards Act provision that prohibits workers from donating free labor for certain community projects. The student had not anticipated this. He was dismayed to learn that what he had worked so hard to put together was actually against the law.

From that moment on, courses in welfare economics and income distribution and labor policy took on a whole new meaning for him. After college he entered law school, with a deep commitment to labor law.

I find this example striking because I know plenty of talented young men and women who say they want to go to law school. But when you press them hard, most of them can't really explain why. This young man knows why. His entire college experience was shaped by the dramatic interaction between the in-class hours and the outside-of-class hours he spent at college. That interaction changed the classes he chose. His integration of in-class and out-of-class pursuits shaped his thinking about how to be a constructive citizen—and ultimately his choice of career.

This student's critical outside-of-class experience was arranged with help from existing student groups, coordinated and run by fellow undergraduates. His story illustrates how, institutionally, a college can help an undergraduate to integrate the in-class and outside-of-class parts of his life.

## Self-Esteem and Pep Rallies

I recently taught a seminar with seven undergraduates. Each was committed to a future career in education. Several hoped to teach, others to do research, others to do policy work. It was a luxurious small seminar—the kind where disagreement among students is welcome, the kind that is sometimes followed by dinner as a group. The kind I enjoy most.

Each student was taking the full undergraduate courseload. Yet most of them also found time to volunteer in a public elementary school in the area. We talked several times about the students' experiences volunteering in public schools. It was clear these experiences had a powerful effect.

In this seminar I created a challenging reading list for the first eleven weeks of the thirteen-week term. I told the students that one of their obligations, in addition to weekly reading assignments and regular essays, would be to help create an additional reading list and writing assignments for our last two weeks. Several colleagues and I often organize our seminars this way, and we find it remarkably effective for engaging students with classwork throughout the term.

That term, the students who were volunteering in the public school urged the entire seminar to explore readings on a certain topic they had all found troubling in their volunteer work. They wanted to read about and discuss ways of enhancing self-esteem for adolescents and preadolescents. Their interest in this topic arose from their experiences as school volunteers.

They believed that the school was working hard to help many children raise their self-esteem, and that the school's leadership meant well. Yet the way the leadership chose to do this was with lots of classroom discussion about self-esteem and self-respect. Eleven-year-old after eleven-year-old stood up and said, "I am smart. I can do anything. I am somebody." My seminar participants called these "pep rallies." They understood the purpose very well, and were not opposed to this if it was part of a broader, more substantive plan. Yet they were deeply disappointed. They could not find teachers encouraging children to tackle a hard task, and to persevere, and persevere, and persevere, with assistance and encouragement, until the children genuinely mastered that task.

My students wondered if the school leadership had it backward. They believed that true self-esteem comes from actually mastering something. The three nonwhite students in the seminar argued this case with particular passion. All drew on their own childhood experiences. The result was substantial reading for the last two weeks of our seminar on the psychology of self-esteem. The students concluded that teaching perseverance to young people is often hard, yet that what increases children's self-esteem is precisely the sustained work that is often necessary to accomplish anything

19

difficult. Children know when they have worked hard, and when they have learned to do something well. That is what develops real self-confidence. Pep rallies are no help at all. My students decided this for themselves in their out-of-class experiences with volunteering, and the reading and discussion in the seminar helped clarify it in their minds.

## Ballet, Turkey Bones, and Surgery

For this final example, I'll let the student tell her own story, which illustrates not only the power of connections between classwork and other activities but also the value of good advising. Here is a somewhat condensed version of what she said in her interview:

I arrived at college having done lots of ballet. I was also into biochemistry. So I decided to focus on chemistry in classes, and joined the College Ballet Group. I wanted to continue dancing and performing, but I found myself developing small injuries, like stress fractures. And I noticed this was happening to some other women dancers. So I began to wonder why. The only thing I could think of was excessive stress on dancers' leg bones. I happened to mention to my advisor what was happening, and he made a suggestion that changed my life.

"Why," he asked, "don't you take your ballet dilemma and explore it in your coursework?" He then suggested I should consider applying for a Research Program grant. It would cover some research expenses. He led me to think how to find a professor to help me explore my question about the impact of stress on dancers' leg bones.

Well, I did it. I identified a professor in the biology department who was studying the effect of orthopedic stress on bone development. I approached him and explained how my outside-of-classes activity, ballet and dance, was motivating me to dig far more deeply into the biological structure of bone development and bone injury and trauma. I told him about two biology courses I had already taken in my first year.

The biology professor agreed, but with one caveat . . . since he was currently working on pig bones, would I be willing to work with him to understand the impact of trauma on pigs' leg bones? It was a start.

Sophomore year, I was constantly working to overcome my leg injuries and get back to ballet. And that was when I decided to make a critical transition: to biology as a concentration, and to turkeys in my research. I designed a project to examine the effects of exercise on bone growth in five turkeys. Real, live turkeys. And as I began to understand what I was doing, the professor introduced me early during junior year to another professor, who was initiating a project relating orthopedic surgery to bone growth. So now I was spending evenings and weekends examining microstructural changes in the bones of turkeys. My family couldn't believe this was happening.

When I decided I would do a senior honors thesis, both of my faculty mentors introduced me to a third professor, a surgeon. And so as part of my honors thesis, I was actually performing surgery on vertebrates, beginning with turkeys, at the Medical School. Because of all these projects, I finally decided I wanted to become an orthopedic surgeon. I have applied to several medical schools.

My outside commitment to ballet gave my academic work a kind of focus and purpose that ended up meaning a lot to me. And I got to know three professors well while doing this. And of course I feel I really know why I want to go to medical school, why doing a certain kind of surgery has special meaning for me.

Whichever medical school I end up attending, I will be incredibly well prepared. And maybe even more important, that decision is based both on lots of information and on real experiences as an undergraduate. I know most people don't find pigs' bones and turkey legs particularly exciting, but for me it was an unbeatable experience.

In short, students who are able to integrate the in-class and outside-of-class parts of their lives can reap great benefits. Those of us who run or teach at colleges routinely talk about financial aid packages for students. It should be possible to help every student to build an "educational package." Rather than saying "Let's admit good students and not get in their way," we should admit our students and then get in their way, in the most constructive sense, to help them make these powerful connections.

# 3

## SUGGESTIONS FROM STUDENTS

Much of what students tell us in interviews can be helpful to others who are wondering about choices they may face in college. Will study habits that worked in high school also work in college? With heavy academic demands, will I have time for activities other than studying? Won't such outside activities hurt my grades? What if I don't do well in my courses—can I get some help? What if my roommates are very different from me? Students have much to say about all these topics, based on their own experiences both good and bad.

## Managing Time

Things that worked for me in high school, I discovered, don't work for me in college. I really was unprepared for the amount of material that is presented here and the speed at which it is presented. It was a bit of a shock. Things I picked up quickly in high school I couldn't pick up so easily any more.

Here at college I wasn't being checked every day. I did not get off to a great start because I had never really learned to study this enormous amount of material in a systematic way. I tended to do one subject for a big span of time and then neglect it for a week. Then I moved on to another subject, and forgot about that for a week. So there was no continuity within each course. That had a lot to do with it. Finally I figured it out. This year, I'm pushing myself to spend a little bit of time every day on each subject.

Why is it that some undergraduates make the transition from high school to college smoothly, while others have much more trouble? Do certain behavior patterns tend to differentiate students who succeed quickly, making superb academic and personal adjustments to college, from seemingly similar students who do not adjust as well?

To pursue this idea, Constance Buchanan and a group of colleagues from four universities devised a detailed protocol to interview two groups of sophomores in depth. (The quotation that opens this section is from one of their interviews.) One group had had an outstanding first year in all ways, both academic and social, while the other group struggled. The interviewers' goal was to explore how each of the students, as a newly arrived freshman, had thought about making the transition from high school to college. They hoped to find a few important differences between the two groups of sophomores. They quickly discovered that one difference, indeed a single word, was a key factor. Sophomores who had made the most successful transitions repeatedly brought up this word on their own. Sophomores who had experienced difficulty hardly ever mentioned the word, even when prompted.

The critical word is *time.* Sophomores who had a great first year typically talked about realizing, when they got to college, that they had to think about how to spend their time. They mentioned time management, and time allocation, and time as a scarce resource. In contrast, sophomores who struggled during their first year rarely referred to time in any way.

Several advisors have told me that some first-year students find it a real challenge to allocate their time so they are both happy personally and effective in their academic work. Students who learn to manage their time well are often those who work hard on this topic when they first arrive. It isn't easy for every student. It requires systematic effort. But the heavy demands of most college courses, compared with what students faced in high school, reinforce the value of making such an effort. It certainly beats the alternative of feeling overwhelmed when suddenly facing the amount of reading assigned in college courses. When seniors are asked what advice they would offer new arrivals, this idea of learning to manage time is a common response. I think it is a wise one. The distinction in attitudes toward managing time translates into a distinction between new students who prosper and those who struggle.

## Balancing Academics and Other Activities

A sophomore told Buchanan and her colleagues:

> Everything here is so fast paced. I forget sometimes, but what I do here in a day is what an exciting month would have been for me back home. It's really intense. And I think I don't realize it until I go home for vacations and sleep until one o'clock in the afternoon. I forget how in high school I used to go to bed at 10:30 P.M. and wake up at 8:00 A.M. Here you're going to bed at 1:00 A.M. and waking up at 8:30—I have a class at nine every morning. And you're going from class, to study group, to my part-time job in the library, to meals, to friends, to performance. It's been a big adjustment.

Each year when new students come to me for advice, I

pass on some of what I have learned from their predecessors: I encourage them to take full advantage of the university community. Above all, I urge them to *get involved* in depth in at least one activity other than courses. It can be paid employment if they need to earn money. It can be an activity with other students, or perhaps athletics or volunteer work. Many of my advisees understand this, but a few need convincing. New students want to do well, and some are nervous when they first arrive. For a few students, their idea of life at college is to sit in classes for twelve to fifteen hours each week and spend the rest of their time studying alone in their rooms.

Some of these students are not very happy. There is a risk they will spend too much time alone. Whenever I see this pattern developing, I raise the issue. Their response is nearly always the same: "My academic work is my priority, and doing other things will hurt my academic work."

Thanks to findings from an extensive survey of Harvard undergraduates directed by Thomas Angelo, I and other advisors now know how to answer such students. We now have concrete data on how outside-of-class activities relate to academic success. The big finding is that a substantial commitment to one or two activities other than coursework—for as much as twenty hours per week—has little or no relationship to grades. But such commitments *do* have a strong relationship to overall satisfaction with college life. More involvement is strongly correlated with higher satisfaction.

Here is a brief overview of students' outside-of-class commitments. These are findings for just one campus. The situation on other campuses may differ somewhat, yet I expect the main relationships, which point to a strong conclusion, will hold up.

First let's consider *paid work.* More than half of all Harvard undergraduates work part time for money, regardless of their academic focus at college. More women work than men. Older students work more than younger students.

They work at an enormous variety of jobs. The most common by far is administrative/clerical, followed by research/data analysis. Women are more likely to have clerical jobs than men. Men are more likely to have custodial jobs than women. The most common time commitment for students who work is between seven and twelve hours per week.

A steadily increasing number of undergraduates work in computing and technology. Many do this for their own learning, separate from paid employment. And for a growing number (now approaching 55 percent), their task on the job is either to help develop new technologies or new applications of existing technologies or to help others on campus apply technology to their work.

There is no significant relationship between paid work and grades. Students who work a lot, a little, or not at all show similar patterns of grades. The grade distributions of students whose jobs have flexible schedules are almost identical to those with less flexible schedules.

Students who work and those who don't work express identical levels of satisfaction with their overall college experience. Workers' ratings of the "overall quality of their courses" are similar to those of nonworkers. Workers' ratings of "overall satisfaction with the challenge level of courses," are similar to those of nonworkers. Responses are also similar for "overall satisfaction with relationships with friends," and "satisfaction with romances."

Two striking findings pop up when students are asked to describe their satisfaction with work experiences. First, on average, the more hours per week a student works, the happier he or she is with work experience as an integral part of college. Second, three-fourths of all working students say that working has a positive effect on their overall satisfaction with college. Only 6 percent think work has a negative effect. Women are even more likely than men to report that work has a positive effect.

What about *extracurricular activities*—outside-of-class commitments not including paid work or intercollegiate athletics? For these the participation rate is 80 percent: 86 percent of women and 76 percent of men. Part of this gender difference is due to men's heavier commitments to intercollegiate athletic teams. This gap has shrunk dramatically in the last ten years as women increasingly participate in intercollegiate sports.

Seventy percent of all students are involved in two or more activities, and 14 percent are involved in four or five. Of those participating in any extracurricular activities, 68 percent invest more than six hours per week on average, and 34 percent spend more than twelve hours per week.

As with paid work, there is no significant relationship between participating in extracurricular activities and academic performance. Students who participate and those who don't have similar grade distributions. Even students with heavy involvement do not have significantly lower grades than those who are less involved.

Another type of out-of-class involvement is *volunteer work*. In any one semester, 25 percent of all undergraduates are involved in volunteering. More than 65 percent of all students do volunteer work at some point during college. Women volunteer somewhat more than men, and upperclassmen are significantly more likely to volunteer than first-year students. Students who work for money somehow find time to do volunteer work more often than those who don't work for money.

Volunteers typically spend between three and six hours per week at their activity. The average is just over five hours. Of the volunteers, 46 percent work with children and teens, 13 percent with the homeless and the poor, 9 percent with handicapped people, and 10 percent with senior citizens.

Why do students volunteer? They report that they "enjoy helping others," or they "want to give something back," or they "want to make the world a better place." Of students now volunteering, 96 percent plan to continue doing so in the future.

As with paid work and extracurricular activities, there is no significant relationship between volunteering and grades. On average, students who do volunteer work have slightly higher grades than those who don't. When asked how volunteering affects their grades, students report no negative impact whatever. When asked how volunteering affects their social life and overall satisfaction with college, students report that on balance it has a positive effect on both.

With the exception of *intercollegiate athletics*, no extracurricular activity is associated with lower grades. Intercollegiate athletes at our campus have slightly lower grades on average than non-athletes. From explorations on other campuses, I believe this finding is widely true. Among athletes, there is also a modest but clear negative relationship between hours spent on sports and grades. It is important to mention one fascinating trade-off here. While varsity athletes have slightly lower grades than average, they also are, as a group, among the happiest students on campus. They have many friends and feel closely bonded to the college.

To summarize, two main findings stand out. If we aggregate all the non-academic commitments of students, adding up total hours spent on paid employment, extracurricular activities, volunteer work, and athletics, *there is no significant relationship between level of involvement and grades.* Yet *there is a clear relationship between participation and satisfaction with college.* Students involved in some outside-of-classroom activities are far happier with their college experience than the few who are not involved.

## Participating in the Arts

My engagement with the theater, not on the acting side, but on the technical side and choreography, has had an impact on me that I wouldn't have predicted when I arrived as a freshman. It has helped me to establish unexpected connections between what I do at the Dramatic Society, or the Experimental Theater, and academic work. I am a History and Literature concentrator. One example came up when we discussed two recent plays by Edward Albee, and how their organizational structure is so different from plays written in the nineteenth century. I had worked hard on producing an Albee play at the Experimental, and it was such a pleasure to share insights about that play with my class.

I don't want this to sound too arrogant, but I think because of my work with drama here I might have actually known more about Albee's writing structure than my instructor, good as she is. After all, I lived it, brooded about it, and had to actually produce it on stage. I think this is what some people mean when they talk about different activities "dovetailing." For me, it all came together thanks to my theater work.

Not every band member became my friend. In fact, I don't especially love many of them. But within a week, since we practiced several times, I found myself making about half a dozen friends. We have stayed close throughout our years here. Between those friends and unexpectedly feeling part of this community the moment I put on my band uniform, it changed my entire sense of well-being.

Many students make a substantial commitment to one or more activities in the arts. Artistic activities are enormously popular at many colleges. Students engage with the arts even more, in sheer numbers, than with athletics and with politics. This is true at nearly every college I have visited. Second to volunteer work, it is the most popular area for students' outside-of-class activities.

If we define the arts broadly to include music, singing groups, orchestra, chamber music, dance, and dramatic productions, nearly half of all undergraduates at Harvard participate at some time during their college years. If we include writing, directing, producing, and doing tech work for programs of music, theater, and dance, the proportion rises to over half. When undergraduates track how they spend their time, about 35 percent find that engagement with the arts is the activity that takes the biggest hunk of their outside-of-class time. This includes planning, tryouts, rehearsals, and actual performances.

Students are enthusiastic about "the incredibly active arts scene" on campus—and I have found similar enthusiasm on many campuses. They characterize the arts as an important source of both pleasure and learning. Since certain kinds of involvement in the arts offer any student at any college the opportunity to build connections between academic work and extracurricular interests, it is worth discussing why students find engagement with arts activities so special.

First, for many students they serve the classic function of sheer pleasure. This pleasure has nothing to do with connecting, say, music outside of class with the formal study of music in classes. It is done for its own sake. Something that takes an undergraduate's mind away from intense academic work. Hundreds of students report that singing or acting or directing or dancing or playing a musical instrument is simply fulfilling, a joy, a release, a "very different kind of creative activity from writing a research paper."

A second reason given by students builds more specifically on how the arts can help to make connections between in-class academic work and outside-of-class activities. A remarkably large number of interviewees mention connections between their own pleasure in the arts and their formal classroom work. Directing, or acting in, or "tech-ing for" a play by Anton Chekhov or Arthur Miller helps students develop insights that transfer to academic work. Their experience with drama leads them to think more deeply about writing, about history, about psychology, about physical environments, about literature in specific contexts, than some might from just reading a play for a class. Similarly, understanding the context and background of music that a member of the orchestra is performing, complete with the context of the composer's life and perhaps the composer's culture, gives many students insights to enrich their academic work. Connections emerge, sometimes unexpectedly. Not for all students, but for some.

A third finding is that a significant fraction of students who participate in the arts report learning certain things about themselves. Sometimes what they learn is unexpected. And sometimes what they learn shapes what classes they choose, their excitement about these classes, and occasionally even what careers they decide to pursue after they graduate. More than a few students report in their interviews that a combination of engagement with the arts and formal academic work shaped their "next steps" in life.

This idea of the arts connecting to classwork is a recurring theme. Some students report that a certain kind of performing, such as drama or singing, opened their eyes to new possibilities for their own future work—possibilities they simply had not thought of before. One example is a young man who tried out for and joined one of the *a capella* singing groups in his first year. He knew he had a good singing voice, yet he was hesitant to perform publicly. By participating in the singing group, he not only overcame his hesitancy, he came to genuinely relish this public performance. He stayed with the group for the next three years, and senior year he became its president. In his senior year he applied to graduate schools of public policy and public administration. He was now considering a career in elective politics. It was performing with the singing group that had given him new personal confidence.

A fourth reason students find arts activities so engaging is that such activities offer special opportunities to interact with, and ideally to learn from, fellow students who come from backgrounds unlike their own. Some of the best interactions, and the most powerful learning experiences, occur when students work together to achieve a common goal. Often at college this happens around a common academic pursuit. But activities in the arts offer a remarkably similar opportunity—a chance to work with people who may be different in countless ways, including academic interests, yet share a commitment to producing a superb play, concert, or ballet performance.

A number of students bring up this point with special enthusiasm. They say that working with others in the arts, more than any other specific activity, has enabled them to benefit from, and learn from, their extraordinarily diverse and talented fellow students. The result is that these students report a high level of engagement, and satisfaction, with their overall college experience.

Even more impressive numbers of students say that by participating in arts groups, especially in the performing arts, they learn about themselves—their strengths, their weaknesses, their interests. And especially how to integrate active commitment to the arts with the college's intense academic demands. In coursework, the task is to do a professor's readings and assignments. You work hard, and you learn a lot about physics, or history, or economics, or literature, but not necessarily so much about yourself. If learning about yourself is an integral part of education, engaging with the arts offers a critical and unique opportunity.

## Getting Help When Needed

> I can't expect the faculty to read my mind, so in the end it really is up to me to take charge of this. My message to other students is simple. Unending help is available, but you have to ask for it. I learned an important lesson. Don't keep academic problems a secret. Unfortunately, it took me far too long to learn it. I hope others with my dilemma figure this out more quickly.

Why do some students perform significantly less well than expected? Reflecting on three questions may help students understand their own situation, and may help their advisors know how to help them. First, are there certain problems that are not unique to any one student, but that are shared by others who are also having academic trouble? Second, what can advisors do to help students who are struggling? Third, what can the students do to help themselves?

While interviewing students, we searched for patterns of adjusting to college, and choices students make, that lead talented people to struggle. We turned up two symptoms of students in trouble and four possible explanations for that trouble. I am confident they characterize many campuses across the country.

## SYMPTOMS OF TROUBLE

It is easy enough to identify certain students about whom faculty and advisors should be concerned—those with distressingly low grades. But they are just the tip of the iceberg. There are two other symptoms that, while less easy to identify, may well be predictive of troubling outcomes.

One symptom, a warning flag, is that a student feels a sense of isolation from the rest of the college community. A handful of undergraduates may relish such isolation, but only a handful. With a bit of effort, an advisor can spot isolated students. They are not involved in any extracurricular activities. They are not members of a study group in any of their courses. And they deal with their low grades by going from classroom to dorm room, closing their door, and studying, studying, and then studying some more, nearly always alone. If their grades don't improve as the year progresses, they don't change their behavior pattern. They just do more of the same, stay up later and later at night, or, in a few cases, simply give up on their coursework.

The second symptom is unwillingness to seek help. Many students show little hesitancy in seeking help from a professor, a departmental advisor, a teaching fellow, or a residence hall advisor. Most universities and colleges have their own organizations designed to provide help.

Yet more than a few students are hesitant to ask for help. And if a student who is having trouble does not seek help and avoids sharing problems with an advisor or professor or teaching fellow, it's hard to give help. Our interviews with forty sophomores who were struggling drove home this point sharply. Of the twenty students who were struggling yet were able to share their problems and to seek help from one of these many sources, all, *without exception*, were able to work at developing strategies to improve their academic performance.

But most of the twenty who were unable to share their problems remained distressingly isolated. They became caught in a downward spiral of poor grades and lack of engagement with other people at the college. It was far harder for them, struggling alone, to turn their situation around.

As the interviews revealed this repeated pattern, my colleagues began to work on concrete suggestions for reaching out to students, even to those students who might be initially resistant to getting help. We met with some success. Four particular sources of potential trouble, and suggestions for helping students to help themselves, emerged from this work.

## REASONS FOR ACADEMIC TROUBLE

One source of trouble is poor management of time. Several of the sophomores with poor grades were studying so inefficiently that they themselves were taken aback when they described their study habits to our interviewers. The single biggest trouble with time use for nearly all students who struggle is their pattern of studying in a series of short bursts. Instead of spending sustained periods of time engaging with their coursework, they squeeze in twenty-five minutes between two classes. They stop by the library to read for thirty minutes on the way to dinner. They begin writing long essays, or working on problem sets, for the next day's classes after coming home from a full evening with a drama group, or sports practice, or singing rehearsal. They are tired before they start, and a long night lies ahead.

This failure to dig in and engage with one piece of work in depth for hours at a time is hurting these students enormously. But the way they organize their time never seems to include longer stretches for serious engagement. Anyone who does much writing knows how difficult it is to do effective and serious writing when the hard work is forced into ten minutes here and fifteen minutes there. This sort of time allocation simply does not enable most people to produce excellent written material. And while this may be obvious to most faculty members, interviews reveal that for a large proportion of students in academic trouble, it is not so obvious at all.

A second source of trouble is that many students who struggle continue to organize their work in college the same way they did in high school. For the lucky ones, this works. For others, especially those who were academic stars in high school but at schools that made only modest demands upon them, this strategy can lead to big problems.

Some students have great difficulty developing new study skills. It is just too easy to continue, locked in, using old patterns. One crucial skill that students must constantly refine is "critical thinking": the ability to synthesize arguments and evidence from multiple sources, sources that often disagree. Nearly all of the students who were having academic difficulty pointed out that their high schools did not demand much of this type of thinking, but that at college it is a crucial skill.

Compounding the problem for students who are struggling academically is their observation that most of their fellow students make the adjustment from high school to college without much difficulty. Watching their friends and classmates and roommates develop certain skills that elude them is maddening. A first-year student described the frustration:

All four of us in my rooming group are taking economics. I would say we are all about equally smart, I know we have similar SAT scores, and we discuss the material sometimes in the evening. Yet they were getting A's and I kept getting C's. I just couldn't figure out why.

Finally, it was driving me nuts, so I went for help. My resident advisor asked if she could see my notes from that class. She looked them over carefully, and then asked me a few questions based on those notes. She helped me to realize that I was great on "giving back the facts," but not so good at all at extending those facts to new situations. Yet here at college, all the questions on exams are about new situations. This is unlike my high school, where all the questions involved simply spitting back the basics.

There is no point in blaming the high school. It just took someone here to help me refocus how I study. Now I understand what the goal of the whole enterprise here actually is. I still am not getting A's, but at least solid B+'s. I don't know what would have happened if I hadn't asked for help and had just continued using that old high school style.

A third source of trouble for some students is their selection of courses. Nearly without exception, students who are struggling, or who are dissatisfied with their academic performance, are taking nothing but large, introductory courses. When asked why they made these choices, nearly every student offers the same response: "to get my requirements out of the way." Clearly, a few students arrive at college each year with the belief that making the most of their experience here involves a sequence of steps. Step one: get all the requirements out of the way. Step two: choose a concentration or major. Step three: take advanced courses in the concentration, while saving electives, the "good stuff," for junior and senior year.

Adopting a strategy of getting the required courses out of the way may work fine for some students. But nearly all students who were in trouble reported that they had chosen this strategy. Since many of the basic required courses have large enrollments, they make it possible for any student to become distressingly anonymous. No professor with a class of hundreds of students pretends to be able to get to know each student well. This is a special dilemma at any large university. Students who choose their courses in this way may rarely engage seriously with a faculty member throughout their first year at college. It is important to stress that this characterization applies to only a small number of students. Yet for this small number, even if it is just 5 to 10 percent of all students, the quality of their academic experience is diminished.

Another disadvantage of using freshman year to simply "get the requirements out of the way" is that students may not find courses that truly engage them, that excite them. The result is that by the end of freshman year (or by sophomore year at many colleges), when it is time to choose a concentration, a student may not yet have been "turned on" by any discipline. The majority of students who followed this strategy of "getting the requirements out of the way" when choosing courses in freshman year regretted having done so.

A fourth source of trouble is a particular study habit shared by almost all students who are struggling academically: they always study alone. Students point out that those who always study alone are isolating themselves from a key benefit of college—the opportunity to learn from fellow students. Fortunately, studying with other students is a suggestion that is relatively easy for a faculty member or an advisor to make to any student. I hope students who read this will decide for themselves to work cooperatively, at least some of the time.

This idea of working cooperatively outside of classes may be new to many students. Indeed, it is new to many faculty members, who went to college when students' working together outside of classes was forbidden, was considered cheating. Chapters 4 and 6, on especially effective classes and especially effective professors, expand on this suggestion and give specific examples.

## Choosing Living Arrangements

With whom should I live? On a residential campus, nearly every student must answer this question. And the decisions students make play a critical part in how they experience college. Thinking through this decision in a careful, systematic way will be an investment that yields high dividends.

A South Asian senior talked about this issue with interviewer Anna Fincke:

Freshman year we had a big mixture. We were six people: Jewish from New York, Jewish from Boston, WASP from Orange County, California, another Indian from Florida, Chinese from California, and me. It was a real mixture in terms of racial background, economic background, and interests. We had all different concentrations: engineering, economics, biology, biochemistry, physics, and social studies. We all wanted to become different things: aerospace engineer, lawyer, doctor, businessman.

We became such a family. That's been one of my most valuable experiences here. I got sick in March and they treated me like my mother would. One guy woke me up every two hours to give me medicine. They were running all over the place, talking to my teachers. And they didn't think twice.

We were really a family. We had a big common room, and we would spend a lot of time with each other, laughing, making jokes. We still have reunions. It was a very meaningful experience. Diversity was central to it all.

The guy from Orange County was conservative, traditional, came from a WASPy family. We butted heads, so to speak. Politically, we'd be battling. He had some religious right leanings. I'm pretty liberal. We would argue or debate. I really like him as a person. It's good to consider someone my good friend who has such divergent views. Enlightenment about other cultures doesn't often come in an epiphany like that.

The first people new students meet, the first day on campus, are their roommates or suitemates. These roommates are assigned by the college; students do not choose their own roommates for first year. At Harvard, first-year students usually live in groups of between two and four. Often, because of the architecture of the first-year dormitories, two groups of suitemates push open a door, keep it open, and informally become a larger "living group" of four or six or eight.

The next group of people new students meet, while they are moving in, are other first-year students who are simultaneously arriving and moving into their entry. At Harvard each student lives in an entry. An entry consists of a dormitory door that leads to a group of rooms and suites, which typically house a total of between fifteen and twenty-five students. This group of students in an entry is assigned to a proctor, usually a graduate student who lives in that entry. This proctor, when all goes as it should, invites all students in the entry to gatherings. These gatherings may focus on simply getting acquainted, or sharing general information, or holiday and birthday celebrations. Sometimes they focus on discussion of academic topics, such as helping students think about how to choose academic majors and concentrations.

Harvard has had such living arrangements for many years. Almost without exception, students describe their first-year rooming experiences as setting a tone for their interactions with other students from backgrounds different from their own. A majority of rooming groups include some ethnic diversity. And every undergraduate lives in an entry that has substantial ethnic diversity. As a result, from the moment a student arrives and puts down the suitcases, the abstraction of a "diverse undergraduate community" comes alive as he or she immediately sees, interacts with, and begins to go to meals with students from a broad range of ethnic and racial backgrounds.

The tone has been set. And this immediate exposure of

every newcomer to people from different backgrounds—from that moment of arrival, to the first meals together, to the first dormitory entry meeting, to all the Freshman Week activities—is what nearly all students characterize as the single most critical, positive first step. It is critical for helping each student feel part of a community. A community with fellow first-year students who look different, and bring different interests and perspectives to campus, and with whom the student will be living, day in and day out, for an entire year. This tone and spirit inevitably become a natural part of college life.

Why do students bring this up over and over as such a big deal? For two reasons. First, they believe the college is sending a message, loud and clear: the message that living with a diverse group of classmates, day and night, weekdays and weekends, *from the outset,* is a standard, important, and, we all hope, enjoyable aspect of coming to this college.

The second reason so many students consider this first-year roommate planning so important is that whether or not any particular undergraduate chooses to continue to live with his or her first-year roommates in ensuing years, an overwhelming majority describe the first-year living experience as a positive one. And the learning that flows from ethnic diversity is repeatedly characterized as an important component of that experience.

As a result, the most frequent suggestion from students is to continue to embed diversity, in a planned, purposeful way, into first-year living arrangements. Doing so sends a message about an idea the college leadership considers important. It leads to surprises. Sometimes it leads to stresses, but usually those stresses are worked through and result in significant learning. In some cases, it leads to lasting friendships that students might never have made otherwise.

Evidence that students respond positively to this policy of embedding diversity into first-year living arrangements comes from their choices of roommates for future years. Interviewer Shu-Ling Chen has found that after freshman year, when they have entirely free choice of roommates, students often decide to live with a remarkable array of friends. For example, several students described to Chen, in late spring of their first year, the living groups they had chosen for sophomore year:

A white man planned to live with another white man, a man from Russia, a Haitian man, two Asian-American women, a black woman, and a Lebanese woman.

A Hispanic man planned to live with "two blacks, six whites, a Pakistani from London, and me."

Another Hispanic man was going to live with one other Latino, three whites, two blacks, and an Asian-American.

A Chinese-American woman planned to live with fourteen others: one other Asian-American, one black, one Hawaiian, one deeply religious Jew, and ten other whites.

A conclusion seems clear. When given an opportunity to choose whom to live with as an upperclassman, a large fraction of undergraduates choose a diverse set of friends and roommates. They report that their choices are influenced in large measure by first-year experiences with their roommates and dormitory neighbors. The assignment of first-year roommates and neighbors shapes whom they meet and whom they come to know. Their strong suggestion to those who design first-year living patterns—it is close to unanimous—is to keep in mind that initial living arrangements can and do shape all future social interactions, especially inter-ethnic social interactions.

# 4

# THE MOST EFFECTIVE CLASSES

Choosing courses each semester is a decision that inevitably shapes a student's academic experience. Two correlations consistently turn up as strong and positive. First, the correlation between the number of small classes any student takes and his or her self-reported personal satisfaction with the overall academic experience is about .52. That indicates a very strong relationship. Second, the correlation between the number of small classes taken and a student's actual grades is .24. This is a lower number, yet it still sends a clear message—that most of the time smaller is better, with stronger student engagement.

When I ask undergraduates what they view as "small," the most common answer is fifteen or fewer people. Two special circumstances deserve a quick mention. One is an independent study or reading course, one-to-one, with a professor. Many colleges and universities offer some version of this luxury. The other is the small seminar.

For many undergraduates, an individually supervised reading or research writing class is the capstone of their academic work at college. A research paper must be written. Supervision is personal and intense. The student gets to play a major role in shaping a project. These are all great strengths for learning, for engagement, for pleasure.

As students tell it, one-to-one supervised research courses are the most intense of all academic experiences. There are no other students to dilute the interaction between student and supervisor. And while most first-year students are probably not ready for such intense research experiences, juniors and seniors advise incoming students that whatever else they do at college, they should not miss the opportunity for one-to-one supervised research.

A small seminar is usually organized in an entirely different way, and for different purposes. Here, since students get to discuss and argue about topics and ideas with one another, the instructor's role is more as a facilitator for productive discussion. One student puts it this way:

> Sometimes I can learn as much from my fellow students as from the professor. This is less true of certain fields, such as introductory courses in languages, where a certain amount of lonely sitting by oneself and learning the vocabulary and grammar is necessary. But it is especially true for both the humanities and social sciences, where four students will have four different interpretations of Thucydides, or Rousseau, or John Locke. A group of students is bound to disagree about what any of these philosophers would have thought of different interpretations of justice in a modern constitutional republic.

Students describe each of these formats—one-to-one research and small seminars—as having its own advantages. They urge other undergraduates to try to choose courses that will allow work in both formats.

## Outstanding Small Classes

A student interviewed by Constance Buchanan and her colleagues recalled a class that really worked:

I had a freshman seminar in the fall that is sort of an ongoing experience that shaped my following year. I have lots of strong memories about the class. One of the best things is how the professor had each of us write a short review of the book we had read for that week. Then we entered into the discussion using that review, and became a resource person for the entire class discussion. Each week the professor would meet with whoever was doing the review, over lunch or dinner.

He got to know each of us on a one-to-one basis. Our interactions were really substantive. We each had three paper assignments and he would write really detailed, two-pages-long analyses of our papers. Then he met with us individually afterwards. That was quite something. There is no large class where the teacher can give that sort of attention to what each of us was doing. The best part is that not only was he devoting lots of attention to me, but I really got to know him as a person too.

As they begin each new course, what do students hope to get out of it? Details vary, but the most common hope students express is that each class, by its end, will help them to become a slightly different person in some way. This hope transcends the subject matter of a class, or a student's background, or even whether the student is a wise old senior or an incoming freshman.

Two factors stand out in students' reports of how small classes make an especially strong impact. First, such classes enable a professor to get to know each student reasonably well. Second, a professor can use certain teaching techniques that are hard to implement in large classes.

When asked which small classes are particularly effective, many students mention a certain organizational technique that faculty members use: organizing classes around some sort of *controversy*. Anne Clark asked undergraduates about their most memorable small classes. Many described classes in which the professor created opposing arguments and built homework assignments that pitted two groups of students against each other on opposite sides of an argument.

Whether the topic is rent control, or foreign aid, or euthanasia, this technique holds great appeal for students. They report that structured disagreement brings out the best ideas from both sides, and that student engagement is high. Many report that the students who are assigned to argue a particular perspective meet outside of class to try out their arguments. So if a professor's goal is to engage students, this idea of structured disagreement holds promise. Students, in turn, may wish to seek out classes that include this format. Those who have already done so recommend it highly.

There were eight of us in an advanced seminar on analysis of structure in literature. The professor said she had attended a symposium where the author Ward Just said: "In my books, I always make sure readers know by about page thirty-five how each of the key characters earns their living. I just think this is critical to help each reader put all the characters in my writing in a context."

My instructor then assigned two books for us to read for the next week's seminar. One was by Ward Just, and it was organized exactly as promised. The other was by a different writer, who is very famous but obviously couldn't care less whether readers ever learned how characters earned their living. Each of us was asked to come prepared to either agree or disagree with Mr. Just's idea. We weren't divided into debating teams—we were each asked to make up our minds. But it was clear the professor was hoping for some disagreement.

Well, she got it. Three of us took the same position as Mr. Just. The other five strongly disagreed. And about a half-hour into the discussion, which was as spirited as we had all semester, one of the women said she couldn't help noticing that the three who shared Mr. Just's view just happened to be the three men in the class, while the five who disagreed happened to be the five women. "Does that imply anything?" she wondered. Which, as you can easily imagine, quickly led to an even more spirited discussion about how gender of both author and reader might influence the way we think about the structure of writing.

Professors with small classes might find this idea worth trying. Students report a simple format: the instructor gives a reading assignment for the next class and invites students to be prepared to make a case for one side or the other of a carefully defined controversy.

One example comes from an economics seminar. In a seminar on welfare and the economics of poverty, ten students were divided into two groups of five. All ten were given several reading assignments for the following week's class on analysis of regulations. One group was asked to come prepared to argue in favor of urban rent control for lower-income tenants. The other group was asked to come prepared to make specific arguments against rent control. Because of the debate format, the students had to work cooperatively in preparing for the next class. They had to anticipate the opposing side's arguments.

One veteran of this seminar found the most challenging part of the whole process to be the homework assignment that followed. The instructor asked each member of the group arguing for rent control to write a paper making the case against rent control, and each member of the group arguing against to write a paper in favor. The students considered this a perfect payoff for the hard work they had done preparing for the debate.

Several students reported this particular example with gusto. When small seminars work well, not only does great learning take place, but they are far more demanding than most larger classes.

## Powerful Homework Assignments

At the outset of this tutorial, there is not a doubt in the world I would have chosen to work alone on any project, wherever possible. No hassle. Do it when I want. How I want. I don't have to worry about what other people think, or their workstyles. Now, after this tutorial experience, I would give the opposite answer for most situations. The wisdom and the amount of work and the arguments that developed in our small group taught me a whole new way of getting a job done. And the biggest message I want to share is that teamwork ultimately depends almost entirely on human connections.

I bet some adults who do this all the time don't realize, or maybe they forget, how hard this is to learn. Look at what I had to learn, in addition to all the substantive economics and methods of analysis, in order to become an effective member of this small working group. I had to learn how to criticize constructively. I had to learn how to argue constructively. I had to learn how to say I disagree with someone's else's idea constructively, even if I secretly think the idea is idiotic.

Most of all, each of us in the group had to develop *trust* in one another. We actually began to feel like a small community. It was wonderful. I had never felt that before about any academic task—partly because I always worked alone on such tasks.

Most college catalogues describe academic requirements as four courses per term. When it comes to workload, these same catalogues and brochures typically say each student should be prepared to spend two to three hours studying for every hour in class. And in fact we have learned that Harvard undergraduates, who spend about twelve hours per week in formal classes, spend approximately thirty hours per week outside of classes studying, reading, writing, and preparing homework.

I find it fascinating that in faculty discussions about curriculum and course structure, despite this inside-outside time allocation, 90 percent of our discussion focuses on what material and ideas to cover in class. We pay far less attention to the details of homework assignments. So it is good for faculty to learn from students that the design of homework, and how we ask students to do that homework, matters a lot. Two relatively small modifications in how homework is assigned and how students are asked to complete it lead to major differences in students' engagement and learning.

We asked some graduating seniors this question: "Which courses had the biggest impact on your learning, why was this impact so big, and exactly how were these courses structured?" The results were eye-opening. We learned that *how* students study and do their homework assignments outside of class is a far stronger predictor of engagement and learning than particular details of their instructor's teaching style. The design of homework really matters.

Specifically, those students who study outside of class in small groups of four to six, even just once a week, benefit enormously. They each do the homework, independently, before they meet. Their meetings are organized around discussions of the homework. And as a result of their study group discussion they are far more engaged and far better prepared, and they learn significantly more.

This finding turns the way an entire generation of professors designed homework assignments on its head. When I was in college, homework assignments had clear rules. Faculty routinely announced that homework must be done independently. No discussion. No talking about it with fellow students. In fact, it was generally understood that collaboration on homework assignments outside of class was a form of cheating.

Now, assuming that faculty change the way they assign homework, and that students change the way they do the homework, professors will be sending precisely the opposite message. Instead of discouraging cooperation outside the classroom, they will encourage it. Instead of considering it a form of cheating, they will recommend it as a way to enhance learning. So acting on this finding will require some professors to rethink a fundamental assumption.

I can report some changes on my campus because of this finding. One change has come in classes in the sciences. Introductory science courses used to be organized the way they are in most colleges, the way they were when I was a student. Undergraduates had regular problem sets to hand in. Quizzes were given. Exams were given. And how students studied outside of class was left up to them—except that they were usually expected to do it alone.

These days, introductory courses in several fields, especially in the sciences, do things differently. Professors not only mention the value of study groups outside of class; some of them actually create such groups. They don't take attendance when such groups meet. They don't insist that every student participate in such groups. But there is a clear, unmistakable change in the way students perceive they are invited, encouraged, and indeed often expected to study for their courses.

Furthermore, many faculty members have restructured their homework assignments so they are actually designed for groups. An instructor may assign, not just chapters in a textbook, but also study questions to guide the reading in preparation for class. These study questions may be far too complicated and elaborate for any one person to answer effectively. So groups of students clearly benefit by working together, getting ready for the next class and discussing their work in advance.

I should point out that for some classes it may be inappropriate for students to do particular assignments in a group. In certain situations the traditional go-it-alone format may be clearly preferable. Yet with so many students reporting that working in small groups enhances their engagement with course material, it seems constructive for any professor to at least consider building a few such assignments into his or her classes.

Students bring up one more point about working in groups outside of class. They feel strongly that evaluation of their work should hold them accountable as individuals. Students who extol the virtues of going over homework problems for chemistry in small working groups over dinner simultaneously point out that each of them still must demonstrate his or her learning individually. Each sits alone and takes several in-class quizzes, three in-class hour exams, and a final exam. In the end, each student must show that he or she really does, as an individual, know the stuff. They do not advocate a group grading process. They simply suggest that since working collaboratively outside of class helps so many students engage with and really learn the material, professors may want to consider proactively encouraging this form of collaboration.

## Courses that Emphasize Writing

Of all skills students say they want to strengthen, writing is mentioned three times more than any other. Most know they will be asked to write an enormous amount at college. Most expect this to continue after they graduate. When asked how they work on their writing, students who improve the most describe an intense process. They work with a professor, or with a writing teacher, or with a small study group of fellow students who meet regularly to critique one another's writing. The longer this work-related engagement lasts, the greater the improvement.

Alumni reinforce the special value of writing. Robin Worth, as part of her doctoral thesis, surveyed alumni from the class of 1977, people now in their forties. One of her questions was "How important is each of the following skills to your *current* work and endeavors?" She then listed twelve skills, such as "use quantitative tools" and "lead and supervise people." More than 90 percent of the alumni ranked "need to write effectively" as a skill they consider "of great importance" in their current work.

Faculty members agree about the importance of writing. When asked what aspect of students' growth they would like our research to cover in depth, a large number chose writing. We therefore explored students' writing experiences in a survey of 365 undergraduates. In a nutshell, the findings confirm that writing plays a pivotal role in the academic lives—and the academic success—of most students.

We also asked sixty graduating seniors to offer specific suggestions to faculty members, and to their fellow students: When are undergraduates most receptive to writing instruction? What kinds of writing instruction do they consider most helpful? And what kinds do they find least helpful?

## WRITING AND STUDENTS' ENGAGEMENT

We asked the 365 undergraduates to describe the courses they were currently taking. Three questions in particular yielded revealing answers. First: In relation to your other courses, what is your level of *total time commitment* to this course? Second: What level of *intellectual challenge* does this course pose to you? Third: What is your level of *personal engagement* in this course?

Interviewers also asked how much writing was required for each course. True, five pages in a history course is not exactly equivalent to five pages in a biology course. But aggregating over dozens of classes gives a general picture of how students deal with different writing demands.

The results are stunning. The relationship between the amount of writing for a course and students' level of engagement—whether engagement is measured by time spent on the course, or the intellectual challenge it presents, or students' level of interest in it—is stronger than the relationship between students' engagement and any other course characteristic. It is stronger than the relation between students' engagement and their impressions of their professor. It is far stronger than the relationship between level of engagement and *why* a student takes a course (required versus elective; major field versus not in the major field). The simple correlation between the amount of writing required in a course and students' overall commitment to it tells a lot about the importance of writing.

Consider a few key findings. First, courses with more than twenty pages of final-draft writing per semester draw nearly twice as much time as courses with no formal writing assignments (an average of eleven hours work per week versus six hours). The more writing required, the more time students commit.

Second, students relate the intellectual challenge of a course to the amount of writing it requires. More writing is highly correlated with more intellectual challenge.

Third, the impact of writing assignments on students' self-reported level of engagement is dramatic. Certainly most faculty members want students to engage with their courses: they may want to keep this finding in mind.

## THE STRUCTURE OF WRITING ASSIGNMENTS

Many instructors routinely ask students to write a certain amount—say twenty pages of final draft over one semester. But how do those in especially effective courses structure their assignments? For teachers who plan to require twenty pages of written work, does it make a difference if they assign two ten-page essays rather than one twenty-pager? How about four five-pagers?

It quickly becomes clear from students that holding the total volume of writing constant, courses that require more, shorter papers demand more time. The pattern is strong. Students spend about 40 percent more time on average— twelve hours per week as opposed to less than nine hours— when asked to do four five-page papers than when asked to write one twenty-page piece. Aggregated over an entire semester, this difference in hours is considerable.

## HOW MUCH DO STUDENTS ACTUALLY WRITE?

In the first year of our meetings to examine college effectiveness, I invited U.S. Secretary of Education William Bennett to join one of our sessions. I asked him to make a few remarks about his view of assessment and evaluation in higher education. In those remarks, he emphasized that while our theme of assessment for institutional improvement was appealing, he wondered if anyone in our group could answer several basic questions about what our undergraduates actually do. As an example, he asked: "How much, exactly, do undergraduates here write? Does anyone here know?"

His question was followed by a short silence. Several participants assured Mr. Bennett they are confident that students here write quite a lot. "You're probably right," he responded. "But where's the evidence? And notice that I am not asking the hard question—how well do they write? I am simply asking about the level of demands you as faculty place on students."

Well, we didn't know then, but we know now. We can now say several specific things about how much writing undergraduates on our campus actually do. These data exclude students concentrating in the physical sciences, since the writing they do for labs and problem sets takes a different form.

We can now answer a simple question: *How many* papers, regardless of length, do undergraduates here write during an academic year? Seventy-one percent do ten or more papers in a year. Only 6 percent of undergraduates write fewer than four papers each year. And what if, instead of focusing on the number of *papers* required, we ask instead how many *pages* each student is required to write during an academic year? These data (again excluding science concentrators) confirm a similar general picture: 83 percent of undergraduates are required to hand in at least sixty pages of work, final draft, in an academic year. The sixty pages is a *lower bound.* A large fraction of students hand in well over a hundred pages. This finding brings good news for faculty members who believe all students should do significant amounts of writing. Only 10 percent of undergraduates write under forty-five pages in a year.

The findings from our survey dramatize the extraordinary importance that students put on good writing. They reveal that including extensive writing in classes does much to enhance student engagement. Perhaps even more striking is how easy it is to discover, on any campus, how much students actually write. The data were easy to gather and analyze. And they paint a picture of a community of students who not only are committed to strengthening writing—they are actually doing it.

## How to Improve Students' Writing

Some students improve their writing dramatically at college. Others show less improvement. Interviews reveal that those who improve most approach their work in particular ways. Their teachers also help them in particular ways. Sharing these findings allows students, and their teachers, to profit from the experiences of others.

A helpful perspective comes from in-depth interviews with sixty graduating seniors. They commented on their efforts to work on writing over their four years as undergraduates. Three strong suggestions about how to improve writing emerged from these seniors' experiences. Each came in response to a question.

The first question was: When should special emphasis be given to writing, especially to preparing longer papers? The answer from many students is a bit of a surprise. The overwhelming majority argue that the best time to emphasize writing is during junior and senior years. They explain that while at first glance it seems first-year students would benefit most from intense instruction, they believe younger arrivals are still adjusting to many new demands of coursework and college life. The seniors feel that in their first year they didn't fully appreciate writing instruction—even the many who in retrospect believe it was excellent. Most viewed it at the time as "just another course requirement."

In contrast, juniors and seniors have finished negotiating introductory hurdles. The seniors point out that writing instruction helps most when students *want* it. This occurs in junior and senior years, as students face more sophisticated demands for research papers. The seniors emphasize that they became eager to strengthen their writing—and that they proactively sought help—as they began to prepare long research papers for small seminars in junior year, or for a senior thesis.

The second question was: In what context is writing instruction most helpful? In response, seniors are close to unanimous. They believe they learn most effectively *when writing instruction is organized around a substantive discipline*. The traditional type of writing exercise—"Write a five-page essay about what you did on your vacation last summer"—offers little help. Students urge more writing instruction in a substantive context. Their ideal is to combine writing instruction with writing assignments in a particular discipline. One senior reports that she began to crave writing instruction when her history professor assigned an essay on how the Renaissance began to empower women.

The third question was: What is the most common misstep in writing instruction? Many students zero in immediately on a particular approach they find frustrating and unhelpful. It is not common, but about one in five students have run into it. The frustration occurs when a teacher seems to forget whose paper it is, and begins to change the voice of an essay from the student's voice to the teacher's voice. One young woman comments about a literature course: "The professor meant well and worked hard with me. I did many drafts. But she kept trying to force her perspectives into my essay. At the end I wanted to tell her that her revisions of my work read well, but now it was *her* paper, and that I was now ready to start over with a different topic to write *my* paper."

I invited each of the sixty seniors to describe a turning point in his or her approach to writing. One young man told a useful story. He described participating in a History and Science tutorial in sophomore year with four other students. Early in the semester, the professor gave his five tutees a short assignment. Each was to read a certain recently published article in a scientific journal. The article had some technical apparatus, but many ideas were presented in prose. All five students got the same job: write a four-page paper summarizing the highlights of this research, emphasizing what is new about the findings.

At the next class session, the professor asked the students to read their papers to the group. Our young man reports that he heard what sounded like four descriptions of four different scientific reports. When his turn came—he was last—his text emphasized different points from the preceding four.

The professor then built the class discussion entirely around writing. He pointed out that their assignment was not interpretive—it was to summarize a straightforward physics experiment. He noted that someone who had not read the original paper would be hard pressed to understand from their several summaries what the original paper had said, and why it was important. The senior recounts that this experience taught him the importance of writing precisely. He was forced to think hard about the differences between creative writing, interpretive writing, and analytic or scientific writing.

Another useful story came from a young woman. She said she had come to care deeply about her writing, but she did not consider it outstanding. She remained hesitant to ask professors to look at early drafts of long research papers. She shared her hesitancy with a friend who was a writer for the *Harvard Crimson*, the campus daily newspaper.

The friend told her that, at the newspaper, editors criticize one another's writing ruthlessly. Relentlessly. For many student writers, this tough but constructive criticism is a high point of working on the *Crimson*. The friend suggested that the woman enlist several other friends to serve as a writers' consulting group.

She did it. She and three others began to meet whenever any of them had a substantial writing assignment and wanted to discuss it. The group had only two rules. First, the person who wanted feedback on a paper had to have at least a second draft. Second, the other three students were not allowed to do any word-by-word editing and fixing.

They met approximately once a week. Each of the four students had about six long papers to write in senior year, giving them twenty-four papers to discuss. The woman called this group her "turning point." She said it was by far her most time-consuming obligation at college, yet of all her activities it was the most valuable. She wouldn't have considered missing a meeting. Her enthusiasm was obvious as she told about the impact of this working group on her writing. For her, work that was once frustrating had become a pleasure.

## SUGGESTIONS FROM STUDENTS FOR STUDENTS

As we synthesize the sixty graduating seniors' anecdotes, several suggestions repeatedly emerge.

*Ask specific questions during one-to-one conferences.* Students who ask questions during student-teacher conferences learn far more about how they can improve their essays than students who don't. These conferences can take place in a basic writing course, or in a small seminar, or even in a section of a larger course. Although some students fear they will appear less intelligent if they ask questions, instructors view students who ask questions as more committed to improving their writing than those who don't ask questions.

The word "specific" is key here. Both students and faculty should think hard about this. Abstract suggestions such as "think more creatively" or "try to introduce your main points more imaginatively" do not help most students when they sit down and begin to revise their essays later that evening. Concrete, specific suggestions from an instructor, such as how to begin to implement revisions to improve an early draft, are worth their weight in gold.

*Ask about recurrent feedback.* Sometimes students assume they understand the written comments on their essays, but they get the same comments repeatedly because they don't interpret them the way their teachers do. Students who improve their writing most take a proactive approach when they get the same feedback on two or more essays. They seek out their teachers and ask them to go over the feedback with them to make sure they understand it.

*Ask for specific examples of problems.* Students who improve their writing most make sure they understand teachers' feedback by asking the teachers to point out specific passages in their essays where the feedback applies. Asking teachers to identify problematic passages also helps students know where they need to focus their revisions.

*Get help from others.* Many students find it helpful to get additional perspectives on their essays. Some schedule extra conferences with their teachers to discuss their ideas or their drafts. Others go to a campus writing center, friends, classmates, or roommates for comments. These comments are more likely to be useful if students ask whoever is reading an essay to evaluate specific aspects of the essay or to read it with specific questions in mind.

*Ask for strategies for revision.* Students who don't know where to begin revising their essays, or who are unsure about how to revise, should ask their instructor to suggest writing exercises or other concrete activities to help them focus their revisions.

## WRITING FOR FELLOW STUDENTS

Writing, its importance and how to strengthen it, keeps turning up as a major theme for students. Now I want to share a finding that some faculty members may find helpful as they think about planning their classes. Students report that a certain way of incorporating writing assignments into a course has special power for enhancing their learning.

The sixty graduating seniors were asked to reflect on these questions: "Think of all the courses you have taken at college. Which course, or couple of courses, had the most profound impact on you? On the way you think. About learning. About life. About the world. And how were these especially valuable courses organized?"

The major finding is not one I would have guessed. Students identify the courses that had the most profound impact on them as courses in which they were required to write papers, not just for the professor, as usual, but for their fellow students as well.

Several dozen students outlined the process in detail. They pointed out that it works best in small classes. And it applies especially to any class that has several writing assignments over a term, and in which the professor leads class discussion. Suppose the class is a seminar that meets once a week for two or three hours. All students, each week, are asked to do that week's reading assignment. The extra step is to ask several students (say three), each week, to prepare an extra written assignment and to complete it a few days before class.

These three students then photocopy their papers, making a copy for each person in the seminar, and leave the copies in a place where everyone in the class can stop by and pick them up in order to read the three papers before the next session. The papers thus become part of the reading assignment for that week's class. Discussion can then be built around the three students' papers as well as the standard readings that were assigned.

Students from these classes rave about the benefits. First, those who are writing "this week's papers" work day and night to do a good job. After all, their work won't just be seen by the professor—it will be read by everyone in the class.

Second, the student writers learn a great deal from writing for an audience of their peers. Traditionally, when students write papers for a professor, they assume they are writing for an expert on the topic. Therefore they may not bother to explain assumptions or to spell out every argument in detail. Writing for fellow students requires a different approach and a different authorial voice. Several students report that the first time they were asked to do this they struggled for days thinking about how to change their presentation. Writing for a real audience of peers is very different from writing only for a professor to get a grade.

Still other benefits flow from this simple, low-tech idea. Class members make reading their fellow students' work before class a high priority. They know their own turn will soon come, when others will be reading and discussing their work. Since all members of the class are highly motivated to do the reading, and to do it seriously and in depth, class discussion is greatly enriched.

Several seniors bring up yet another benefit of sharing papers in advance. They say that seeing fellow students' work opens their eyes to new possibilities. They feel empowered in their own work as they see for themselves, often for the first time, that different ways of presenting an argument can work well. Many add that in addition to seeing different styles of writing and presentation, they become able to distinguish different levels of excellence.

Notice that this format capitalizes on the principle of students' engaging with faculty, and with one another, around substantive ideas and academic work. When students' papers are read by the entire class, an overview of different styles and arguments that used to be available only to the professor now becomes available to each student. Most love it.

## The One-Minute Paper

We asked faculty members and students what single change would most improve their current teaching and learning. Two ideas from both faculty and students swamped all others. One is the importance of enhancing students' awareness of "the big picture," the "big point of it all," and not just the details of a particular topic. The second is the importance of helpful and regular feedback from students so a professor can make midcourse corrections.

Most colleges and universities use a course evaluation form that students fill out after each semester. Information from these forms gives useful data to faculty—how well particular topics are received, how well various classes are organized, which textbooks are most helpful, what problem sets lead to the best learning. But typically a professor gets all this information after a course is over. That is helpful for next term, but not for next class or next week. Many faculty members point out that feedback *during* a course, when immediate changes and midcourse corrections are still possible, is even more valuable.

Patricia Cross, now a professor emeritus of higher education at the University of California at Berkeley, suggests a simple and low-tech device called the one-minute paper that addresses both the emphasis on the big picture and the need for feedback. The idea is to conclude the regular class lecture or discussion a minute or two before the end of class time. Then ask each student to take out a sheet of paper and write down, *anonymously*, brief answers to two questions:

1. What is the big point, the main idea, that you learned in class today?
2. What is the main unanswered question you leave class with today? What is the "muddiest" point?

A box is placed near the door to the classroom, and students drop their papers into the box as they leave. The professor picks up this bundle of anonymous papers and spends five minutes or so riffling through them. As Pat Cross points out, "You will be surprised at how quickly you will learn exactly what the students understood, what wasn't so clear to them, and you may even get some good ideas about how to begin your next class, in response to these one-minute papers."

This extraordinarily simple idea is catching on throughout Harvard and at many other campuses. It invites student reflection and feedback. Some experienced professors comment that it is the best example of high payoff for a tiny investment they have seen in years of teaching.

One of my colleagues, a master teacher at Harvard's Kennedy School of Government, recently began to use the one-minute paper in his classes on economics. He believes an unspoken but important side benefit of the one-minute paper is that knowing they will be asked to fill out the paper at the end of class focuses students' thinking. Students are constantly asking themselves, "What is the big idea here?" and also, "What is unclear to me, and how can I write a few coherent sentences that convey what I don't understand?" They are thinking throughout the class about what they will write. So this low-tech exercise keeps students' minds focused in a helpful way.

My colleague adds that starting each class with a quick overview of responses from the last session's one-minute papers builds continuity over time. It also offers a comfortable way for him to clear up any misunderstandings. Several colleagues note that students appreciate the opportunity to give immediate and specific feedback to their professor, especially when a particular class session doesn't go well.

Frederick Mosteller used the one-minute paper in his courses on basic statistical methods. He even extended it a bit, adding an additional step. After each class he wrote up a brief summary of information from the students' one-minute papers, which he handed out at the next class. Students found this handout particularly helpful. Not only did the professor get quick feedback on what was clear and what needed more work; students also learned from the summaries of their responses. Each student could see what the entire class found clear and unclear, and also whether his or her particular question was shared by many others.

In an article entitled "The Muddiest Point in the Lecture as a Feedback Device," Mosteller describes how this innovation changed his teaching. He estimates that it took him about an extra half-hour per class to prepare the summaries: "In all I prepared six handouts that I would probably not otherwise have prepared, along with two more that I probably would have prepared anyway." And about six minutes at the beginning of each class was spent responding to queries. In addition, the class ended a couple of minutes early so students could do the paper. In all, about 15 percent of the class time (in 53-minute classes) was changed.

And what of the students? Mosteller says:

A few who seemed not to have a class in the next period pondered their responses for exasperatingly long periods while I waited, and they seemed very satisfied with what they had written. I did not have the impression that anyone prepared a response before coming. Nobody complained to me about lecture time lost. And of course, if you believe that participation speeds learning, as most people do, this task raised the level and maintained it at each session. (Mosteller 1989, p. 16)

To summarize, the one-minute paper has many benefits. It may not be suited to all courses, but it beautifully fulfills Robert Wilson's (1986) list of four benefits for any valuable teaching innovation:

1. It requires more active listening from students.
2. It helps instructors identify students who need special help or who lack adequate preparation for the course. In the best case, it helps students identify for themselves how they are doing.
3. It improves and focuses students' writing. Responses during the last weeks of a class are longer and more thoughtful and articulate than those during the early weeks.
4. It helps document for students that they are indeed learning something substantial in the course.

## Myths about the Physical Sciences

Many of my faculty colleagues want to focus attention on the sciences. They are aware of a growing national concern that too few students are specializing in science. A corollary is that students who don't specialize in science know too little about scientific topics. What can we learn from student reflections on their experiences with science classes at college? At Harvard, each undergraduate must take a minimum of three such classes. What are their experiences? Do they have constructive suggestions for faculty members?

One clear finding from our studies is that misperceptions about science classes abound. A small number of myths, none based on evidence, are constantly mentioned. These perceptions have a great impact on who does or does not choose courses in the sciences. Let's take a quick look at six common perceptions, some of them more accurate than others.

The first perception is that *most undergraduates are not interested in work in the sciences when they first arrive.* This perception is wrong, at least on my campus and probably on many others as well. Math, the physical sciences, computer sciences, and engineering taken as a group have more students expressing a strong interest in concentrations than any other group of courses. This is true both for men and for women. It is true by a large amount.

The second perception is that *students are frustrated by science faculty members' emphasis on research.* This perception is also wrong. Actually, it is nearly backwards. Several years ago, of sixty students asked about this directly, only seven expressed this view. The other fifty-three disagreed, many of them strongly. About half of these fifty-three said that a big point of coming to this college is precisely that the faculty does cutting-edge research. Their hope is to participate in it and help with it, at least as upperclassmen. They did not come here to avoid it.

A follow-up examination of this same question led to similar results. Forty-two of fifty seniors concentrating in the sciences said directly that they would not want to work with faculty who were not actively pursuing their own research. One student put it this way:

> Of course, I want a faculty advisor who is a good
> teacher, who is kind, who is willing to spend time
> supervising me, who is available, patient, and who explains things clearly. But if to get that level of perfection
> I had to work with a faculty member who was not actively doing research, I am not sure why I would seek

such a person out to supervise me. My goal is not just to learn biology. It is much more than that, especially by junior and senior year. It is to learn how to really *do* biology. And it seems pretty clear to me that to do biology I need to learn from someone who is actually doing it too.

Yet all is not perfect. It rarely is. About half of these same fifty students reported working closely with a faculty advisor. The other half reported getting some supervision, but they wished for even more.

The most successful students got extensive supervision in two ways. One was working with a professor in that faculty member's lab research, often as part of a team. A big plus of this experience is the collegiality with fellow students, and occasionally additional faculty members, who work on such teams. A second form of supervision came from writing a senior thesis. Twenty-four of the fifty students who were interviewed identified writing their senior thesis as the peak experience of their academic learning at college. Without exception, they were proud of their work. When asked about the trade-off between working with faculty who emphasize teaching and working with those who emphasize research, nearly all of these twenty-four students said they found that an unnecessary choice. They described faculty with active research programs as generally the most compelling teachers.

The third perception is that *many undergraduates avoid classes in the physical sciences because they worry they can't do the work—their backgrounds and prior preparation are strong in humanities, but not in math and science.* This perception is half wrong. Of all students who take only the minimum number of math and science courses required by

71

the college, approximately 30 percent express worries about their preparation. The other 70 percent are quite confident they can do the work. They choose classes in fields other than science for other reasons.

The fourth perception is that *students who avoid science classes have thought through their decisions carefully, and later are glad they made them.* This perception is partly wrong. Nearly all students think carefully about their course choices. But not all juniors and seniors are entirely comfortable with their decisions about science classes.

One interview question brings this out. Students concentrating in the humanities were asked, just before graduation, "What is your one biggest academic regret?" The question was asked in an open-ended format, inviting students to say just about anything they chose. The single most common response, with no prompting from the interviewer, was, "I wish I had taken more science." We got this response from 39 percent of the humanities concentrators. While I don't know how students at other campuses might answer this question, students at many schools might benefit from reflecting on these regretful responses from thoughtful seniors.

The fifth perception is that *many students avoid science classes because the workload is significantly heavier than for classes in other fields.* This perception is in some measure correct. According to student ratings of workload summarized over dozens of courses in different topic areas, natural science classes indeed have heavy loads. But they are on average tied with classes in languages. And their workload is rated just slightly higher than for humanities and social science courses.

The sixth perception is that *there is more grade competition among students in the sciences than in other areas.* This perception is clearly correct. Summaries of student ratings for competition for grades in five different course areas tell a clear story. Science classes stand alone, well above the other four areas.

## Suggestions for Science Faculty

From several rounds of in-depth interviews, four insights emerge about circumstances under which students especially appreciate and engage with science classes.

### WORKLOAD AND GRADE COMPETITION

First let's focus on those students with strong math and science backgrounds who avoid science classes at college. A key reason given by many for avoiding science classes is the heavy competition for grades. It is tempting to question the sincerity of such responses. Maybe some people don't want to do the hard work of science classes, and are using excessive competition as an excuse.

Fortunately, we have empirical data about courses with heavy grade competition. They are taken from a recent set of course evaluations. For the fifteen natural science courses that students rate highest in overall quality, it is easy to compute the average student ratings of their grade competition, and also of their workload. Similarly, for the fifteen lowest-rated natural science courses, it is easy to do the same two computations. The findings confirm students' responses in interviews. The fifteen highest-rated courses are described as having only modest grade competition, while the fifteen lowest-rated courses are described as having considerably more grade competition.

These differences are just barely statistically significant. But that is not really the point. The point is that students' perceptions of good science courses focus on those with modest rather than higher levels of competition for grades. A cynic might suspect that students are criticizing grade competition when in fact they are frustrated by courses with heavy workloads. To examine this, we can compare the workloads of the top-rated fifteen science courses with those of the bottom-rated fifteen. Such comparisons show that the workloads for the two groups are virtually identical. In fact, the courses with *less grade competition* are described as having *slightly heavier* workloads. But this small difference is not statistically significant.

What can a science professor infer from these findings? It appears that when students say they are declining to choose science classes because of intense grade competition, not because they fear a heavy workload, they are telling it straight. It is worth considering whether classes can be structured so that students who are put off by intense grade competition—generally those who are not science majors—will be less put off.

## SMALL STUDY GROUPS

Small groups appear to be even more important for the sciences than for courses in any other field. Whether or not students work together in small study groups outside of class is the single best predictor of how many classes in science they will take. Those who do work in small groups take more science courses.

Any professor can implement this idea quite easily. Whether the class has ten students or two hundred, a professor can encourage students to work in groups outside of class. Indeed, a professor can even *create* the groups if students seem hesitant to do so themselves. The key to these groups' success in the sciences is that they should meet *after* each member has done the problem set, or lab assignment, or readings for class. Meeting beforehand is far less productive. By meeting afterward, the group can focus on unanswered questions and challenges that came up during each student's solitary work. An increasing number of faculty members in the sciences are encouraging their students to meet outside of class and to review their work on homework problems in this collaborative manner.

## INCREASING INTERACTION

One suggestion was brought up by more students than any other: *substantive work in the sciences should be structured to involve more interaction with other students and with faculty members.* Many perceive serious work in the sciences as impersonal. In contrast, they think of classes in humanities and social sciences as "dealing with people— their real-life dilemmas, their joys, their tragedies, their conundrums," as one woman who switched from chemistry to anthropology put it.

When I mentioned this point to faculty colleagues in the sciences, one responded, "But physics and chemistry and biology are beautiful and rich and deep too—just in a different way." I know this. And some students know it too. But unless professors make a conscious effort to share their perceptions of this beauty, they will continue to lose some students. And the most promising way to share such perceptions, according to students who have chosen to work in the sciences, is to build small work teams so students interact more. For example, create a discussion group after each major lab experiment. That way, rather than going home alone into the night, students can immediately share findings, frustrations, and surprises with others. They become part of a continuing conversation among young fellow scientists.

Some faculty members may feel perplexed by this suggestion. What does it have to do with training a student to become an outstanding scientist? Students understand that small-group discussions after a lab experiment add only marginally to the hard-nosed science in their repertoire. But the small groups accomplish something else that students report is crucial—they build collegial spirit, in a collegial community. And that is crucial for success in the sciences too. Students long for it.

When undergraduates describe instruction in science classes, they repeatedly mention those professors who already work to create such small communities of young scientists. It is always with respect and thanks. One student described such a teacher as "the adult who has had the biggest impact on my academic work, and on me personally."

## HOW TO ATTRACT AND KEEP MORE STUDENTS

One of the misperceptions I discussed earlier is that most students arrive at college with little interest in studying science. The data show otherwise. Many first-year students on many campuses express a strong interest in doing some work in science. Substantial numbers plan to concentrate in science, including computer science and applied math.

A large fraction love the experience. They work very hard. They feel challenged. And many choose science as a lifelong commitment. In contrast to this happy group, however, a significant minority enter college with a strong background and plans to emphasize science, but soon switch away to other fields.

When asked to describe how they approach their work, students from these two groups sound as if they are describing different worlds. Those who stay in science tell of small, student-organized study groups that meet outside of formal classes. They describe enjoying intense and often personal interaction with a good lab instructor. In contrast, those who switch away from the sciences rarely join a study group. They rarely work together with others. They describe class sections and lab instructors as dry and, above all, impersonal. Each night they go back to their rooms and study alone.

As mentioned earlier, science professors who succeed in structuring their classes and labs to help undergraduates work collegially are praised by students. The word "inspiring" is used often. These professors attract specialists in both sciences and other disciplines to their classes. Their success is not due to some mysterious charisma, or to their entertainment talents. It is due to the way they organize the work in their courses.

## Foreign Language Classes

Few incoming first-year students are even considering concentrating a substantial part of their work in a foreign language or literature. The majority of freshmen, when asked directly, express neither special interest in nor dislike of languages. For many, learning a foreign language is simply a requirement, to be gotten out of the way as painlessly as possible.

My visits to dozens of other campuses make clear that such lack of interest is widespread. When asked directly to explain this perspective, more than a few students comment on the quality of the foreign language teaching they received in high school. Often it was not from native speakers of a language, and often it was the narrowest type of rote learning.

Yet when undergraduates at Harvard do pursue language

studies, for some a sort of personal transformation takes place. With the exception of tutorials, these classes are rated higher than any other group. These ratings take into account how students value a course overall, and also the quality of teaching. Students report that language courses have extremely heavy workloads, yet for most of them, interest in the subject matter is high.

And these ratings transcend any particular language or group of languages. Whether it is the Romance languages, or Germanic languages, or Asian languages, or Slavic languages, or Classical languages—all of these are singled out by juniors and seniors as classes in which they feel they grew significantly. And for 60 percent of students who take them, these classes are described as "hard work but pure pleasure."

My first thought on seeing these responses was that students treasure having specific skills—skills they can immediately put into practice—and that foreign language classes quickly give them such skills. But then I found that ratings for advanced courses in foreign literatures, taught fully in the foreign language, surpass even the high ratings for basic language courses. These ratings defied easy explanation. They also led to a series of further interviews with 335 undergraduates, and questions to 670 alumni, focusing specifically on foreign languages and literatures.

The major finding is that students who take such courses end up committing enormous amounts of time to them. Yet they report overwhelmingly that their heavy commitment is repaid many times over by their accomplishments. They take special pleasure from simultaneously exploring language and literature.

We found that students arrive at our campus with strong backgrounds in foreign languages. Nearly all the students surveyed could have placed out of the language requirement and taken no such courses at college. Yet in an early survey only 31 percent exercised their option to skip advanced courses, and more recently that has dropped to about 25 percent. Half of all students here pursue one foreign language or literature, and 20 percent now pursue two or more.

How do students decide which languages to pursue at college? After all, most students were limited in high school to whatever few languages their school offered. The overwhelming majority choose to continue studying the language(s) they began in high school. A modest number (16 percent) continue a language from high school and also begin at least one new one. An additional 12 percent study an entirely new foreign language, a complete change from whatever they took in high school.

Do most students get helpful advising about foreign language and literature studies? At least at Harvard, the answer is no. In fact, this negative response stands out sharply. Only 12 percent of students report having received helpful advice about choosing courses in foreign languages. I have no systematic data about quality of foreign language advising on other campuses. Yet from visits to many, my strong impression is that many other campuses are similar to Harvard in this respect.

## ADVICE FROM ALUMNI

Alumni have strong views about their work in foreign languages and literatures when they were undergraduates. Within ten years after graduation, a significant number have extended their own expertise: 28 percent of young alumni have studied one foreign language since college, and another 16 percent have studied two or more.

Their advice to current undergraduates, boiled down to its

essence, is this: take as many language courses as you can. An impressive 94 percent of alumni say this. Different respondents express their suggestions in different ways. A majority, 57 percent, urge students to take courses in foreign languages and literatures "even if you officially test out of the requirement." Twenty-one percent urge students to find a way to spend time in a country where the language they study is spoken. Another 16 percent urge students to take more than one foreign language. Only 6 percent disagree, urging students to test out of taking any foreign language if possible.

## EXPLAINING THIS ENTHUSIASM

I believe the big message from these findings is that students are enthusiastic when classes are structured to maximize personal engagement and collegial interaction. Languages don't receive such great compliments for some inexplicable, mysterious reason. Explanations for this praise emerge quickly from students' qualitative responses.

How do they describe language courses? Usually class sizes are small. Nearly all are under fifteen, and many have fewer than ten students. Instructors insist that each student contribute and speak up regularly—even those who are shy. Students are encouraged to work in small groups outside of class. The classes demand regular written assignments, generally essays or exercises each week. And frequent quizzes give students constant feedback, so they can make repeated midcourse corrections. In sum, these classes are already putting into practice exactly the features that students describe as most valuable for enhancing their engagement with coursework, and their learning, in *any* subject area. And students love them for it.

# 5

## GOOD MENTORING
## AND ADVISING

Good advising may be the single most underestimated characteristic of a successful college experience. Graduating seniors report that certain kinds of advising, often described as asking unexpected questions, were
critical for their success.

One senior tells about the academic advisor she had
during junior and senior years. This woman is a government major, an exceptionally strong student. She tells of
consulting several faculty members whom she respected,
whose classes she had taken, and who knew her and her
academic excellence. She reports that one person made all
the difference. Here is a somewhat condensed version of
her story:

Each time at the end of sophomore year when I went to
talk with professors about research topics and an honors
thesis, our conversations were very academic, but somehow I was missing the connection between those academic conversations and my own personal values and
convictions.

I was beginning to think about going to graduate school
as a Ph.D. candidate in Government. And I had decided
the price of admission for starting graduate work was that
I had to have something to say. I was determined to avoid
choosing a substantive topic that was so academic it
would be divorced from what I care about in this world.

That is when I met the professor who became my academic advisor. I could tell from our first conversation that he understood my wish to take a stand, to connect the most abstract academic work with making some choices that matter to me personally.

He began by asking me which single book had had the biggest impact on me. I told him it is the Bible. He didn't look surprised at all at that answer. Already things were looking good. Then he asked me to name five authors in my field who had had the biggest influence on my thinking. I told him they were, in no particular order, Alexis de Tocqueville, Aristotle, Edmund Burke, David Hume, and John Rawls. When he smiled and said he was "beginning to get a sense of me," it was like music to my ears. He was the first professor who was more interested in trying to understand what matters to *me* than in immediately discussing the strengths and weaknesses of the Rawls position on justice, with little sense of what this all means to me. After all, if I am going to write a thesis for many hundreds of hours, I want it to have some personal meaning as well as academic excellence.

He asked what areas I wanted to pursue in more depth. I told him it was the dilemma between a politics that focused on the success and welfare of groups, versus a politics that focused on the well-being of individuals. It seemed to me that focusing on this conflict might explain many disagreements in political philosophy in modern democracies. And unlike several other professors, who were wonderful but as a matter of style turned immediately to an abstract discussion of political philosophy, this professor responded with a question. "Did you ever see the David Hare play called *Skylight?*"

Well, not only had I not seen this play, I had never heard of it. He told me, "It's about two people who are confronting exactly your thesis topic. In this play, there is a woman who has left the man she lived with so she could teach low-income children. She tends to think of people as members of a certain group or category. He doesn't know how to do that. The man comes to find her, and in the most dramatic lines of the play, he tells her, 'Loving the people's an easy project for you. Loving an individual person, now that's something different.' Is that what you want to write about?"

You can't imagine how excited I was. Here he not only asked me what I thought—I realized he was making a real effort to "climb into my head." That is what I call a super advising experience.

I should add that he was writing a book on World War II and the Holocaust, and so he was able to point me to people and books that raised questions I had to think about for my thesis. For example, at one of our meetings he quoted Elie Wiesel: "Questions unite people, and answers divide them." Might I, he wondered, find that a helpful way to organize a chapter of my thesis? He gave me lots to think about.

At another of our meetings, he suggested I concentrate on how language can shape a concept or an argument. He cited a writer from the Netherlands, Abel Herzberg. This man is a survivor of a concentration camp, and stresses in his writing that the Holocaust didn't happen because six million Jewish people were murdered, but rather one Jew was murdered, and then another, and then another, six million times. My advisor wondered if this was helpful to my analyzing political philosophies that distinguish between consequences to groups and consequences to individuals.

Maybe it is too much to ask that each advisor put out a special effort to help students connect their academic work with their personal passions. But whenever this happens, I think it must be good. By the way, I should add one last point. Although it took a long time for me to really understand my advisor's personal political views, because he tried to keep them out of our discussions, it turns out we disagree on more things than we agree on. But I think in retrospect that only added to the strength of our work together.

Young women and men arriving at college immediately confront a set of decisions. Which courses to choose? What subject to specialize in? What activities to join? How much to study? How to study? Such decisions are intensely personal. Often they are made with little information. Yet their consequences can be enormous. A subject that is bypassed, or study habits that are mismatched for certain classes, can result in limited options, reduced opportunities, or closed doors. Advisors play a critical role. They can ask a broad array of questions, and make a few suggestions, that can affect students in a profound and continuing way.

## The Power of Good Advice

During more than ten years of research for this book, I visited more than ninety colleges. Some are highly selective. Some are close to open admissions. Most are in between. They include private and public colleges, large and small, state universities and junior colleges. Of all the challenges that both faculty and students choose to mention, good academic advising ranks number one.

Agreement is widespread that academic advising is important. There is also agreement that the best advising is tailored to each undergraduate's unique situation—his or her particular background, strengths, areas that need improvement, and hopes and dreams. But different campuses have widely different resources for advising. A small, private liberal arts college with 2,000 students nearly always will design a different advising system from a large, public state university with 20,000, simply because of different resource constraints.

Several findings about good advising have emerged from our student interviews—findings that may be helpful to advisors on many campuses. And the good news about these points is that they are relatively easy for advisors to share with students and for students to implement.

In particular, one remarkably simple suggestion comes up over and over as students reflect on their own college experience. The suggestion builds on the obvious idea that part of a great college education depends upon human relationships. One set of such relationships should, ideally, develop between each student and one or several faculty members. While I say this is an obvious idea, many new students do not mention this point when I ask about their plans and goals for their college experience. So I bring it up when advising new students.

Each year I meet one-on-one with several new students. And each year our conversations follow a similar pattern. We begin with a discussion of the student's goals at college. Then we move on to a short conversation about the student's background. And then we turn to the main event—a discussion of a "study plan." We discuss what courses the student will take in this first year, and how those may lead to future courses. My special effort is to encourage students to reflect on what courses, taken in that critical first year, will most help them to make wise, informed choices in the following three years. I warn students against simply choosing random classes that sound interesting, with no real idea of how taking certain classes may help them make decisions about future courses, and even about their major or area of concentration.

Then we come to the part of our conversation that I look forward to most. I ask, "So, now that we have had this conversation, what do you see as your job for this term?" Just about all students answer that their job is to work hard and to do well here. I press them. I ask what else might they set as a goal. This time their responses often emphasize participating in campus activities. And again I press them to say more about their goal for the semester.

By now, most students look puzzled. They wonder what I am getting at. And then I share with them the single most important bit of advice I can possibly give to new advisees: "Your job is to get to know one faculty member reasonably well this semester, and also to have that faculty member get to know you reasonably well."

It is clear that most incoming students have not thought about this goal quite so directly. I point out that achieving this goal may require some effort and planning. Yet think of the benefits. Even if you only succeed half the time, I remind each new student, that means in your eight semesters here you will get to know four professors. And they will get to know you. Then I mention a very practical reward for achieving this goal. In senior year, I tell them, when you are looking for a job, or applying to a graduate or professional school, or for some sort of fellowship after college, you will have four professors who can help you, who can write recommendations, who can serve as references.

I have done this with new students for nearly a decade. As my first-year advisees approach graduation, many tell me that this advice was the single most helpful suggestion they got in freshman year. Many of my colleagues now give their own advisees this advice as well. I understand that on some large campuses it may be far harder for students to implement this idea. Yet I would still urge any student to make the effort. Suppose on certain larger campuses a student only gets to know two professors reasonably well in four years, rather than one per semester. I am convinced that student will be far better off, and will have a far richer experience, than if he or she gets to know no professors at all.

## Learning from Successful Students

How can we learn what good advising involves? Since it is not possible to do a controlled experiment, in which one group gets a certain kind of advising and another doesn't, we can try to identify people who clearly succeeded at college. Then we can retrospectively explore what impact a certain type of academic advising might have had on those people. Retrospective analyses can easily be criticized as less than ideal in statistical rigor, especially for making causal inferences from treatment to outcomes. Nonetheless, I had to start somewhere. As it turns out, these conversations with particularly successful students are turning up a fascinating perspective about good advising.

The students I chose to interview were Rhodes and Marshall Scholars. I thought such students, who clearly were highly successful in college, might have some insights and ideas about what constitutes good advising. Clearly some-

87

thing went very right for these students. I asked them, one-to-one and in depth, about the academic advising they received. I have interviewed thirty such students.

One overarching theme emerges: twenty-two of the thirty have mentioned it without any prompting. They say that at key points in their college years, an academic advisor asked questions, or posed a challenge, that forced them to *think about the relationship of their academic work to their personal lives.*

Here I arrive, from my small public high school out west, and probably a bit immature. I had no idea what to expect when I first met with my academic advisor. So I went to our first session very well prepared. I was armed with a list of six possible courses from which I would choose four. I also had a list of questions to ask him about the different sciences, and what focusing on each would require.

To my slight surprise he knew something about me, and he went out of his way to make me feel comfortable. But after greeting me, and inviting me to sit down, he immediately asked "Why are you here?" I thought he meant why had I come to see him, so I started telling him about course selection. He quickly interrupted and said, "No, I mean why are you here at Harvard?"

This was not a question I expected. So I guess I was a bit flummoxed. I told him I had come here to get a great liberal arts education. Then he asked the question that I haven't been able to stop thinking about for all my four years. "Tell me, what exactly do you mean by 'a great liberal arts education?'" I didn't have a good response, but I told him I would think about that question for our follow-up meeting the next week, when he was going to sign my course study card.

I don't want to say what anyone else should do. But I can say that by personalizing our first few conversations, by asking me what my goals are for college, and by pressing me hard on the question of how studying the physical sciences fits within the definition I proudly gave of a good liberal arts education—I never forgot his questions, and those conversations. It would be hard to attribute any particular success I had in any one course to that advisor. But there is no doubt at all that when I reflect on choices I made here, I can still hear his hard question from that first week ringing in my ears.

A common strand from many interviews is that students who interact with their advisors by talking about "bigger ideas" are the ones who find these conversations most helpful. Those who simply use the opportunity to get a quick signature on a study card are missing out on conversations that could change their perspective on what they are studying, why they are studying it, how what they study fits into a bigger picture of their lives, and what new ideas might be worth considering.

An interview with a Rhodes Scholar illustrates what can come from several good advising sessions. This is a young man who concentrated in biology. He planned after his two years on the Rhodes to go to medical school. He told me how his freshman advisor had thrown him for an unexpected loop. The advisor kept pressing him for reasons he wanted to be a doctor, rather than simply signing a course plan. And this young man, sensing that his advisor was helping him in a profound way, kept coming back for more.

My advisor made a real difference. He asked me very

hard questions about why I was doing what I was doing. He asked whether I had thought about alternatives. He pointed out that I could complete all the requirements for medical school and yet concentrate in a more traditional liberal arts field. When I told him my mother had urged me to focus on preparing for medical school, we actually sat over medical school catalogues, and for the first time I understood that I didn't just have to load up on science courses.

As it turns out, my true love is philosophy. Here I am, an African-American, and there aren't too many of us who do philosophy. But the department welcomed me, and so I am officially a philosophy concentrator. I realized that I am using philosophy and some of the dilemmas it raises to understand more fully some of the questions that had led me to want to go to medical school in the first place. For example, I have now done a lot of reading on the trade-offs between extending life and quality of life for elderly people. These readings seem to be pushing me toward gerontology as a future specialty, although I may change my mind.

But the point I want to make is that my advisor kept pushing me to relate my coursework to my own interests. After we had met several times I confided to him about how my interest in medical school began. My mother has severe emphysema. And I believe she hasn't gotten the very best health care. She teaches elementary school, and we aren't rich. So she gets medical services under a managed care plan. Now that she is older, I see that she will struggle to keep a decent quality of life for herself. And I would like to help in any way I can. In retrospect, my advisor's pushing me to relate my work at college to my personal concerns is what encouraged me to do philosophy while preparing for medical school. I am sure I will be a better doctor because of this good advice. And I think I can be a better son too.

## Time Logs

Keith W. Light (no relation to the author) has had great success with an idea that advisors might suggest to all students. The idea is simple. It is to keep a personal time log, recording exactly how time is spent, half hour by half hour, for a certain period.

Implementing this idea has three steps. Step one is to encourage first-year students, on a voluntary basis, to track their time for more than a day or two. Two weeks is the period we use here. Step two is to sit and debrief with each student, one to one, about what their time log shows.

This is somewhat labor intensive: a one-to-one debriefing typically takes about fifteen minutes. Yet I would argue that even if only some first-year students find this helpful, if we amortize those fifteen minutes over a four-year college career, the investment of about four minutes per year per student seems like a high-return proposition, both for the students and for the college.

A third step is to follow up a few weeks after the debriefing, to see if each student is actually implementing whatever insights and suggestions emerged from going over the time logs. A single follow-up call, with encouragement to persist in efforts to implement changes, has made a measurable difference in the lives of some of our students.

Keith Light implemented this simple idea with 173 freshmen. He invited them to track how they actually spend their time, half hour by half hour, for two weeks. Then (with several colleagues) he debriefed each student. The questions asked during the debriefings were predictable, yet personal to each student. "How was your time actually spent?" "Are you pleased with the way you spent each day?" "Are there certain changes you might like to make?" "What is an effective plan to implement these changes?"

It is critical to stress that encouraging students to track their time systematically is just the first step. The debriefing, and encouraging students to implement whatever changes they want to make, is what leads to the payoff. Without discussing the concept of implementation with each student as an individual, the payoff for the substantial effort of keeping these logs may be lost.

One of my faculty colleagues who has worked with time logs, Frederick Mosteller, offers two wise suggestions for any student who does this exercise. First, it helps to think of each day as being divided into three parts—morning, afternoon, and evening. By planning each part thoughtfully, it is often possible to set aside at least one of those three parts to accomplish some uninterrupted work. Second, a crucial focus in the debriefing should be on how time in between scheduled obligations is used. For example, a student with a class from 9 to 10 A.M., and then another class from noon to 1 P.M., has two hours of in-between time.

How should the student use this time? He may choose to chat with friends. He may choose to go back to the room to study. He may want to do a few errands. He may want to do something athletic, or do some physical exercise. There is no single correct thing to do. Rather, whatever he chooses, the key point is that it should be done with some thought.

Keith Light stresses an additional and more personal advantage of time logs. He points out that the process of time logging offers an opportunity for student and advisor to get together. When asked why they don't meet with their advisors on campus more often, some students say they are shy or hesitant to seek out the advisor. Especially when there is no compelling reason, no clear agenda, or nothing that seems urgent to discuss. The time-logging activity and its debriefing session provide natural, entirely unawkward occasions for advisor and advisee to connect.

Consider what the debriefing session accomplishes. For a student, it is a rare chance to reflect together with an adult about how he or she is now allocating time and energy. Is the student pleased or displeased with the current situation? What possible adjustments might the student want to make? How can any adjustments be implemented? Meanwhile, the advisor gets a running start in helping a student. It is hard to imagine a better way for an advisor to get to know a student than by sitting with that student discussing how he or she spends precious time, hour by hour, day by day.

The debriefing offers each advisor an opportunity to get to know his or her advisees at as personal a level as each advisee chooses and feels comfortable with. It is a great chance for an advisor to genuinely advise.

## One-to-One Substantive Mentoring

In a classroom situation, you're the only one who suffers if the work is not your best. When you submit a paper, you know it is an academic exercise for your professor, which he then is obligated to grade. But when you understand how seriously this woman, my mentor, takes her work, and of course, how important you feel it is, you treat each word a little differently. This work will be a chapter in a book. And my mentor hopes this book will become a new standard for the impact of women studying the physical sciences in college, where our investigation is done with the best scientific research designs. So when she asks me to help write up any finding, my choice of words really matters.

It takes on a whole new level of seriousness and commitment. After all, this writing is not just for a professor, or for a grade. We are doing this work together to push forward the chances of women excelling in the sciences. I've just got to figure out, with my mentor's help, how to write up our main findings in the most compelling way possible.

The word "mentoring" comes up often in conversations with students. And I have yet to find colleagues who think it is a bad idea. Yet what constitutes good mentoring?

Interviews with graduating seniors cast some light on the kinds of mentoring students value most. As I mentioned earlier, of all the skills students especially want to strengthen, writing ranks number one. So several interviewers and I asked a random sample of graduating seniors to reflect on their experiences at college, both in and out of class. Could they point to a particular activity that had a particularly memorable impact on their academic development? And especially on their writing skills?

It turns out that many of the students who improved their writing had one specific type of experience in common. They had all worked in a one-to-one, mentored research project with a faculty supervisor.

Our campus offers several informal opportunities for students to participate in such projects. I call them informal because no student is required to participate in such activities and they do not offer any academic credit. Many of these opportunities are to work with regular faculty members, who participate as mentors. Some of the opportunities are to work with visiting scholars or other research specialists. These include visiting research scholars in a science department or at a campus organization, as well as scholars based in various interdisciplinary academic centers. At Harvard this includes organizations such as the Center for European Studies, the Russian Research Center, the Du Bois Institute for African-American Studies, the Latin American Studies Center, and the Center for East Asian Studies. Other campuses have their own organizations.

The list is long. And that is exactly the point. There are enormous numbers of opportunities for students to connect with potential mentors. And our interviews revealed that such mentored experiences, organized outside the regular classroom structure and not done for academic credit, have a strong positive impact on students. A handful of specific experiences make a remarkable difference in students' experiences here.

How do such mentoring opportunities work? An undergraduate applies for a small amount of financial support. He also finds a faculty mentor who agrees to supervise his work, one-to-one. Again, this work is not done for academic credit. And I want to be clear that this activity does not involve a handful of faculty—it involves more than a hundred.

What does this format accomplish? Several things, especially for the students. Each student who lines up a mentor and writes a successful proposal receives a small stipend to serve as a research assistant to a faculty member. This is a wonderful, low-tech, win-win situation. A student gets a bit of extra financial aid. Most can use it. And faculty members get a young colleague to mentor, to work with, on a topic both parties care about. So the professor has little administrative overhead—and most who volunteer to do this describe it as a particularly fulfilling activity.

Faculty participants are asked to attend a one-time session with the program coordinator for these mentoring efforts. The discussion at this session focuses on how each supervisor might want to structure the process. Faculty members talk about what specific steps they might take to make this a memorable, positive experience for students. Many faculty members, including some of the busiest and most distinguished senior professors on campus, volunteer to participate.

Several other campuses I have visited have started similar programs. I believe any student should consider participating if such opportunities arise.

A few quick words to campus leaders. Is such a program of mentored internships expensive? It isn't free. And perhaps not every campus can afford it. But the general size of a grant to students is small, several hundred dollars. Given the level of tuition and general expenses, if a one-time expenditure of this magnitude makes such a difference for student after student, how can we not pursue it? Amortized over four years, the investment is modest.

Let's listen to what some students say about this mentoring program. Here is a senior woman:

> The best part has actually been having a role model. I know that sounds unbearably cheesy but it's so true. Particularly because my mentor is just ten years older than me. So it's been great to have someone who's right between me and my mother. And it has been inspiring to me that in ten short years this woman has really got-

ten her act together and is contributing to knowledge. I simply had no idea how a scientist—she is a biologist—can agonize over practically every word in her project write-ups. Maybe I *should* have known this, but the fact is I didn't. It completely changed the way I think about my own writing.

One afternoon, when we were going over a short draft of findings that I had written, my mentor didn't think the concluding paragraph captured the essence of our findings as well as she had hoped. So I figured she would change a few words, and touch it up. We ended up spending nearly four hours, that entire afternoon, choosing and discussing word choice for that final paragraph. And it was only about six sentences! I never dreamed what impact this experience would have on my writing. I have come to enjoy working at it, and it has been an unending effort. I have no doubt it will continue.

Other students note that in their courses, all the homework, reading assignments, and exams are arranged for them by a professor. That is fine and understandable. Students do not make this point as a complaint. They simply point out how different it is, what a challenge it is, to work on designing their own project. Or, in some cases with mentored internships, to work on actual research. So these mentored projects, done for no formal academic credit, take students out of a classroom setting and put them at the cutting edge of a project. Usually each student gets to shape his or her own project, or his contribution to a larger, group effort. The key point is designing a project from scratch, rather than simply carrying out professors' instructions. This is hard work, yet students praise it as an especially powerful kind of learning experience.

## Getting Involved in Group Activities

All the suggestions so far for students seeking good advising or mentoring have a common thread: each focuses on the academic side of a student's life. Interviews with students who have had academic difficulty turn up one more finding. A non-academic finding. It is that for some students, the single biggest contribution an advisor can make is to encourage them to join a campus organization or group that will give them social and personal support.

Some students from minority groups stress this point. So do students who are the first in their families to go to college. And so do students who are leaving behind crucial support networks they had in high school. Such networks can include parents, especially supportive high school teachers or counselors, religious counselors, athletic coaches.

Our work on advising reveals the extraordinary importance of some sort of support group for each student. A large fraction of students who underperform can be characterized as having left a support group they had in high school—often a support group crucial to their success in high school—without finding a new, similar group at college. These are the students most likely to feel lonely when they get to campus. Such students may not integrate quickly or easily into their new community. For many, their academic work as well as their social life and sense of being grounded will suffer. When this happens, it illustrates how strong the connections are between academic performance and outside-of-class activities.

What is the policy implication of this finding? That advisors should encourage students from their very first days on campus to find a group to join. Step one is for each advisor to simply make this recommendation to each advisee. Not every student will implement this suggestion perfectly. But some will do just a bit more than they might have done otherwise, even if it takes them a bit of time to get their bearings.

Let me give one example in which such advising made a world of difference. A student interviewer talked with a sophomore who had arrived at Harvard from an island in the South Pacific. The sophomore came from a low-income family, and neither of her parents had attended college, nor had her older brother. She had been at the very top of her high school class, but, she told our interviewer, after her first few days at Harvard she was on the verge of packing up and going home. She felt simply overwhelmed by everything. The activities, the pace, the course selection, the big city nearby, even the other students.

When she first met with her advisor, a few days before classes began, he quickly saw that she was overwhelmed. And so, remembering our finding about the connections between academic performance and non-academic activities and the importance of support groups, the advisor urged this new student to find an outside-of-class activity that she would enjoy, ideally one that would also help her get to know other students.

The advisor suggested writing for one of the campus newspapers. The student declined. How about joining the Glee Club? The student didn't think her voice was good enough. Did she play a musical instrument? No, she didn't.

The advisor took his job very seriously. He refused to give up. He listened to her responses, and then made a specific suggestion. When the Harvard Band held tryouts the next week, this young woman should show up and try out. The freshman repeated to her advisor that she did not play any instrument. "No problem," he replied, "just tell them you want to hold the drum."

The advisor happened to know that one of the college band drums is so big that a second person often helps the drummer hold it. In fact this young woman did become a member of the Harvard Band, and this single event was critical for keeping her here. While her grades were good, the dramatic success was her extraordinarily happy overall experience. When our interviewer pressed her to analyze her success, she repeatedly mentioned the band. She got to know many other students well. Also, becoming part of the band, with its performances at football games and other campus activities, gave her a wonderful sense of identification with a particular community, a feeling of belonging.

This young woman told her interviewer that all of these good things had happened because of that conversation with her first-year advisor. She never would have thought of joining the band, and certainly not just to hold a drum. Those few minutes with a wise advisor who understood the importance of a support group for a student of her background made all the difference. This advisor's one insight fundamentally changed the quality and texture of her college experience, including her academic engagement as well as her personal happiness.

## Encouraging Collegial Work

Throughout this book I have emphasized the importance of collegiality. An incident at the beginning of my own graduate student days drove home the message to me.

I arrived at Harvard as a Ph.D. student in statistics. I felt young. I certainly felt nervous. I learned an important lesson my first week here, entirely outside of class, from my advisor. It taught me about the meaning of collegiality.

I checked in at the statistics department a few days before classes began in the fall. My purpose was to make an appointment with the man the admissions letter said would advise me. His name was Frederick Mosteller.

To my surprise he was immediately available in his office. He invited me in. After some pleasantries, I suggested we make an appointment. I had in mind getting some advice about course selection. He quickly agreed. We set a time for later that week. Then, just as I was getting up to leave, Mosteller asked me to wait a moment. He picked up a small bundle of paper, put a paper clip on it, and handed it to me. When I glanced down, I saw that its title was "Non-sampling Errors in Statistical Surveys: A Chapter for the International Encyclopedia of the Social Sciences."

"Richard," asked Mosteller, "could you please mark up this draft for us to go over when we get together later this week? I'd love to get your comments on this."

I was panicked. I hadn't even started my first course, and already my advisor was asking for comments on his work.

The next two days were difficult. I read the chapter ten times. Finally I felt I understood it pretty well. Two days later I returned for our advising session. I handed him back his draft. I told him I had learned an enormous amount from reading it several times. I thanked him for giving it to me. I told him I thought it was superb, and that other readers would learn a lot too.

Mosteller smiled and told me kindly but directly that he had hoped for something different: "I treated you like a colleague, and you didn't do that for me." He explained that by sharing his first, rough draft, complete with occasional typos and grammatical errors and imperfect organization, he was assuming I would help him, as his professional colleague, to improve it. So now, as a colleague, it was my job to dig in and to make specific suggestions.

He said that he always enjoyed hearing compliments, yet my praise was not helping him at all. The way I could be helpful was to suggest how he could improve his manuscript. Mark it up with red ink. The more, the better. That, he told me, is the ultimate contribution of a good colleague. He wouldn't promise to take all my suggestions, but that wasn't the important part. The important part, he said, was that going through the process together was part of becoming a professional.

I took Mosteller's admonition very seriously. I returned a few days later carrying a document covered with red ink. I even included suggestions about writing style, choice of tense, choice of subheadings, and many other details. The payoff came when we had our next session a week later. He put my marked up version on the desk between us, and starting on page one, we went over every suggestion I had made. As promised, he rejected many of my changes. But he took a few. And we had good discussions about many others. Mostly, it was he who did the explaining.

Finally I understood. I realized that what had at first seemed like his request for *my* help, was actually Mosteller's giving me *his* help. He was doing his job. He was advising me. Brilliantly.

He taught me two things. The first is that writing is often a lonely, painstaking enterprise, involving many drafts and a willingness to dump whole sections when necessary. At age twenty-one, that was not obvious to me. Second, he taught me about collegiality, about how important it is to share early drafts without embarrassment. He modeled, with his own behavior, how working and debating with another person about a work in process is a way to pay them a great compliment.

I have never forgotten those lessons. For years I have asked my own new advisees to do exactly the same thing. I share this story because I stay in touch with many of my own former students from the past thirty years. And this one act—sharing a rough draft of a document and asking my new, young advisee to mark it up so we can sit together and discuss it—is what they remember and mention more than any other. They describe it as the single best moment of advising they got. They say it shaped their attitude toward writing and their view of themselves as young professionals.

# 6

## FACULTY WHO MAKE A DIFFERENCE

When asked to estimate their own impact on students, more than a few of my faculty colleagues rate it as "modest." Perhaps for some professors this perception is correct. Yet for others it couldn't be more wrong. They dramatically underestimate their influence on students' overall development. According to undergraduates, certain professors exert a profound impact. They influence students' development as young scholars, as good citizens, as human beings.

This message shines through interview after interview. We asked graduating seniors this question: "Can you think of any particular faculty member who has had a particularly important impact on you? In shaping the way you think about yourself, or life, or the world around you, or your future? If yes, tell us what this faculty member did that had such a strong impact."

Of all students who were asked this question, 89 percent quickly identified a particular professor. They explained in detail how these professors had changed them. And two-thirds of these students wouldn't quit—they insisted on naming more than one faculty member who had been critical to their college life. Only 8 percent of undergraduates could not come up with a professor who had had a major impact on them.

What do certain professors do that particularly matters to undergraduates? As a professor for more than thirty years, I confess I particularly enjoyed students' responses to this question. Some got so involved with their explanations that it was hard to shut them off. One reason so many took so long to give their answers was simply that they had never been asked this question before. And students on any campus are eager to be heard.

The sections in this chapter present the main themes students bring up when describing professors who make a real difference. The best part of these examples is that they rarely depend on inborn or immutable personality traits of any faculty member. Rather, students identify certain planned efforts these special professors make.

I am confident that these findings transcend any particular campus. My own goal in teaching is to make a difference in my students' lives. That is why I chose this profession. I know many of my colleagues, at Harvard and elsewhere, have this same goal. All of us can benefit from the insights students share.

## Teaching Precision in Use of Language

One undergraduate speaks for hundreds of others when he summarizes his appreciation for a certain professor: "I will never forget him, because he never tried to tell us *what* to think. Rather, he worked hard to come up with ways to help us learn *how* to think creatively."

Many students give examples that illustrate *the importance of choice of language.* They note that precision in choice of words can change an opinion and sharpen an analysis. It can even change the way people think. Some instructors make a point to capitalize on this idea, and students seem to remember the particular examples long after their classes end.

My most memorable professor was the young woman who taught my junior year government seminar. The topic was income distribution and redistribution. And her choice of language, which she had obviously thought about a lot, got me to recast the way I think. She actually got me to change my mind. That's an accomplishment. She did it all with choice of language.

She insisted her students try, in class discussion, to avoid ever using the word "government." She reminded us that government has many constructive roles, but that ultimately it is individual citizens and taxpayers who pay all the bills. She suggested that adopting her strategy might give us new ways to think about the role of government. Since my politics tend to be liberal, I was skeptical. But she was absolutely right. Let me give you an example.

During the debates leading up to the year 2000 presidential race, Vice President Al Gore pointed out that for many families with young children, good daycare services are awfully difficult to find. So he proposed that the federal government should pay for additional daycare programs, especially to assist working women who want to find and keep good jobs. I supported that idea strongly. I thought it was close to a no-brainer. In class, I spoke up and used the Gore proposal to illustrate what I considered a constructive role for government.

The professor very nicely asked me to rephrase my remarks, but without ever using the word "government." Instead, she invited me to use the words "my fellow taxpayers."

So I said that I supported Vice President Gore's proposal, and that my fellow taxpayers should subsidize daycare for working women. Then the professor asked a question. First, she asked, suppose you marry, and have a child, and you make the choice to forgo income for your own family because you want to stay home with your young child. Are you sure you want to tax yourself, and other families like yours, for that choice? Do you believe you should subsidize other women who make a different choice, and who decide to enter the work force and earn money that you yourself have chosen to do without?

Put in those words, I was a lot less sure of what I thought. And then the professor really zinged me. She asked, "Suppose you change your mind, and decide you do want to work outside your home. And that therefore you need daycare for your children. How enthusiastic are you about taxing your fellow citizens, your neighbors, such as all the people who live on your street, to pay for your choice?"

Well, that did it. I told her she had raised the question in a way I hadn't thought about before, and I needed time to think.

I can't get the professor's insistence on precise choice of words out of my mind. This professor really did change the way I think. I got to know her pretty well after that class, and I learned that she shares many of my liberal political views. Yet she demanded that I think clearly and rigorously about the implications of my beliefs. And she accomplished this through the choice of language. I especially respect the idea that her demands were neither politically liberal nor politically conservative—just a demand for clarity of thought. From all her students. So that is the professor who had the biggest impact on me.

## Sharing Intellectual Responsibility

One-on-one working relationships between students and professors provide opportunities for students to take some responsibility for planning and running academic projects. These experiences teach students something they may not be able to learn in standard classes.

> During my junior year I did a one-to-one supervised research paper. I arranged that my supervisor would be a young faculty member who has a great reputation as a supervisor. My topic was nineteenth-century European history and literature, special emphasis on Germany and France.
>
> In our first meeting, my supervisor made his expectations clear. By the end of the term, I was to have a paper done, final version, somewhere between fifty and seventy pages. We would meet weekly, and we would take turns choosing the readings for the following week. He pointed out that this format put a substantial responsibility on my shoulders. In my other classes, the professor always chose the readings. Now every other week I had to choose readings that were appropriate for my work. He further reminded me that since I would undoubtedly choose some readings that he had never done before, it was my responsibility to plan our discussions on the readings I chose.
>
> Unlike any course I had taken here before, I was now truly responsible for "course planning." I had to take some intellectual leadership. This was made even clearer when in our first session where I had chosen the readings, my supervisor interrupted me repeatedly with tough questions. I did the best I could, but I could tell it wasn't quite good enough.

He must have seen I was a bit upset, because he quickly stopped and explained why he was doing this. He pointed out that we were truly learning together. He reminded me that my job was to play some part of "student" and some part of "teacher" in these sessions, since it was just the two of us. Honestly, after a while I think I got quite good at it. And being forced to play the role of teacher has made me think that maybe I want to pursue these ideas in graduate school.

Even when I had worked hard and written what I thought was good, I was always pushed to extend myself. To stretch. Whenever I wrote about literature, my supervisor pushed me to put the discussion of literature in its historical context. And whenever I focused on a historical point, he pressed me to do the reverse. I began to think of this wonderful man as my "personal trainer." Just the way an athlete has a personal trainer to constantly press him to run just a few steps faster, to jump just an inch or two higher, I had the academic equivalent of such a guy.

I actually was disappointed toward the end of the year if he didn't press me that way. My father once told me the only way to become a better athlete is to play hard against others who are slightly better than you at the sport. My faculty supervisor clearly knew far more than me, yet asked me to "play the game" and "hold up my end" in the best sense. I learned more in this one-to-one experience, about history, about literature, and about my own capacities to stretch and grow, than in any other experience here I can think of.

This young man honors the professor who asked him, indeed required him, to help build a reading list. This was new for the young man, and it was not easy. Yet as he learned to do it, with support from the professor, he gained a new sense of confidence both academically and personally. I would think any faculty member who is able to work individually with undergraduates might want to consider trying some version of what this professor accomplished. I would think also that a student who wants to really dig in and learn new skills might want to seek out a professor who is willing and able to arrange this sort of a supervised mentorship.

## Connecting Academic Ideas with Students' Lives

When asked to rate courses they take, students often give the most rigorous and demanding classes their highest ratings. Yet from the interviews a fascinating observation emerges about certain faculty members whom students identify as having had an especially powerful influence on their thinking, and on their lives. The faculty members who had an especially big impact are those who helped students make connections between a serious curriculum, on the one hand, and the students' personal lives, values, and experiences, on the other.

Students praise certain faculty members who build such connections into their teaching. I asked the students I interviewed to give one example to illustrate how a professor did this, and then to say why it had such a memorable effect.

A young man told me about his junior-year government seminar. One week the professor assigned John Stuart Mill's "On Liberty." The assignment was to read this classic closely and come to the next seminar meeting prepared for a short quiz on a few key points. This young man said that this seminar had developed several small study groups, in which students met the day before class and organized their own discussion of the major reading.

When they arrived at class, the fifteen students were given the short quiz. Then the professor announced that he believed the quiz had taken care of his obligation to make sure each student was up to date on doing the reading. So now he was going to pose two questions for group discussion, based on "On Liberty." The questions were: "In his writings, John Stuart Mill characterizes those who describe themselves as political conservatives as members of a 'stupid' party. First, why did he say that? What are his assumptions and arguments? And what is the context in which that statement is made? Second, do you agree, or not? Feel free to draw on Mill's writing, on other academic sources, or on experiences in your own life, in your own families and communities, to think through Mill's assertion."

The student reported that conversation in that seminar was extraordinarily vigorous. It was vigorous because the professor's question invited some conflicting responses from students. You could practically guarantee that several students would argue that Mill's insight was perfect, while others would rake him over the coals for faulty generalization. And still others would point out that Mill's idea of the word "conservative" was clearly different from our modern understanding of that word. The young man summarized his enthusiasm about that professor:

Look at what each of us took away from that one, great session. First, to prepare, we read Mill's work carefully. Second, we knew we would be required to participate in the discussion in class. So that meant we had to think through our own positions on Mill's philosophical arguments. Third, we met outside of seminar the day before, to work through our own thinking by discussing it with classmates. And fourth, we got a full sense of the diversity of opinions, and experiences, and interpretations, as presented by the other fourteen people in the room.

I got insights from that single discussion that I remember to this day. The key to it all is that the professor invited, and really encouraged, each of us to draw from our own real-world observations and experiences to enrich the full group discussion. The big thing for me was to see how the backgrounds different people came from have such an enormous influence on the way they interpret the readings. I had never seen it come alive so sharply before.

I remember one student's remarks in particular. They made me rethink my interpretation of the relationship between personal liberty and each person's sense of obligation to community. This is a woman whom everyone else in the class viewed as the most politically conservative person in the group. She comes from a fundamentalist Christian family. In this session she described how both her family and her church had taught her, growing up, a particular sense of responsibility to her community. She felt closely tied to the welfare and well-being of others in her community.

She connected her experience, of growing up in such a family that was basically a minority in their community, with the arguments on community and individual responsibility that are presented far more abstractly in Mill's work. It was all new to me. I had never known anyone who grew up in a family quite like that one. And I couldn't believe the connections she was able to make between the readings and her own life and sense of obligation.

I think that any professor who is able to organize academic work in a way that draws students deeply into the ideas, yet simultaneously invites them to make connections between abstract ideas and their own real lives, becomes an unforgettable professor. The learning that takes place in such a class transcends what I would call purely academic learning, and is really seared into our consciousness. And I stress how I especially appreciate any professor who does this while maintaining the highest academic standards.

And one last point. There is a lot of talk on campus about students learning from one another. I think most professors don't always capitalize on the incredible diversity that students bring to actual classroom situations. What better way to capitalize on it than to encourage students to relate the readings to incidents in their own lives? It seems pretty obvious to me that this approach will deepen each student's personal understanding of what may sometimes seem abstract.

Students will bring different perspectives, experiences, and interpretations to the classroom discussion. The discussion will be richer. I bet we all learn more as a result. I think maybe faculty who can do this will be remembered for a long time by their students.

## Engaging Students in Large Classes

Research universities inevitably have some large classes. Nearly all large classes are introductions to fields, or basic courses such as biology, economics, and psychology. Some students express a wish for fewer large courses.

The chances of eliminating large courses are slight, if only because doing so would be very expensive. So when any student talks about a professor who created a participatory atmosphere in a large class, I take special note. When choosing their courses, students at any college or university may want to look for professors who, even when teaching large classes, still get students actively engaged in what goes on in the classroom.

One senior had strong opinions about this topic. An economics concentrator, he was critical of Harvard for having too many large classes. And an even bigger point, he said, was that too few professors who taught large classes engaged their students actively in their classroom learning.

Asked to give an example, he described his class in behavioral economics. He said that despite the class size, the professor interspersed his lectures and presentations with "in-class exercises" that forced each student to think on the spot. Furthermore, the exercises were structured to teach students something about the behavior of large groups—one of the topics of the course—by using each student's response as part of a large group of responses from everyone in the class.

The student told about a particular class session that focused on understanding the behavior of large groups. The professor lectured about negotiation and an understanding of group behavior as important components of any individual's decisions. After describing rational behavior theory, he stopped talking and pulled a slip of paper out of his pocket. This, he told the class, was a certificate for a free pizza. One person in the room was going to win it.

The professor invited each member of the class to write down any number between 0 and 100. He would collect these numbers and average them, and the student whose number was closest to half of the overall class average would win the pizza. So the class stopped all other activity for about two minutes. Each student wrote down his or her name and a number on a piece of paper and passed the paper to the front. A student in the front row averaged the numbers and then announced the result.

I was not sure I understood the student's point. It was clear the professor was getting everyone in the large class "involved." But why was this so special? My interviewee explained:

That was a powerful learning experience. My first thought was that the only way I could win would be to guess 50 or less. The highest possible average for the whole class is obviously 100, so a guess of 50 would win the pizza. But then I realized that there are lots of very smart people sitting all around me, and they all are thinking the same thing. And if they all think just what I think, and write the number 50, then the winning number becomes 25. Yet of course just as I thought of this point, most other people in the large class will too. So I realized I had to lower my guess, since others will lower theirs. Then it occurred to me that this is an unending, asymptotic process where the lower limit is zero. But that assumes everyone in the large class thinks of this, and assumes everyone else's behavior is rational. So in the end I decided that I would write the number 16.

Well, the whole class was discussing this exercise. We were discussing how each of us thought about it as the fellow in the first row tallied up our group responses. The professor just stood in front, awaiting the results. In about two more minutes, the fellow announced that the average number submitted across the entire class was 22. Since one woman had written the number 11, she had gotten it exactly right. The professor made a big deal out of handing her the certificate for her free pizza. We all applauded, and some of the clowns in the class even stood up and gave her a standing ovation.

That is a class I will never forget. It taught me some principles that are critical in my field. I think most of us in that large class feel the same way. By creating this exercise where each of us had to participate, and forcing each of us to actually write down a number and hand it in, the professor was engaging us actively, and kind of forcing us to put ourselves on the line. For those few minutes, it was as if our large and occasionally impersonal class were in a small-group session. Everyone was debating with their neighbors how they thought about this challenge.

The professor didn't just let this drop after the woman won the pizza. He went on to build an elaborate theory of rational group behavior. And by doing this exercise to motivate it, he had our full concentration, and we understood what he was telling us, and why it could be important. For example, in negotiations of any kind, especially if there are multiple group interests involved, this sort of analysis is valuable. What a wonderful way to teach.

If you are gathering a collection of examples of teaching that make a strong, positive impact on students, feel free to add this one to your collection. Whenever something like this can be worked into a large class, it makes what could be pretty impersonal into a far more personal experience. If you ask me to make a list of professors who have had a lasting impact on me, this man is at the top. He showed me what could be done within the context of a large class.

## Teaching Students to Think like Professionals

All good physics and economics and psychology teachers cover and explain principles of their subjects in classes. The professors students remember most are those who go beyond such principles and are able to convey to students "how physicists think" or "how psychologists think." Undergraduates contrast this ideal with the other end of a continuum—classes in which, say, a psychology professor conveys information in a lecture: "Freud's contribution to psychology is . . . And Skinner helped to create and formalize behavioral psychology, which means . . . And developmental psychology has grappled for decades with the nature versus nurture controversy, where those who argue in favor of nature believe . . , while those who argue in favor of nurture believe . . ."

This sharing of basic information is valuable. Information is important. Students want some of it. They do not argue that classes should be devoid of it. Yet graduating seniors report that if they could do it again they would seek out more classes in which a professor asks questions, or poses problems, that help a student to "learn to think like a psychologist."

An empirical finding supports the value of this approach to teaching: a student's choice of what field to major in is driven more by this than by any other single factor. When a student believes she knows what it means to "think like an economist," she is far more likely to focus her learning in economics.

When students tell me this in interviews, I press for specifics. A senior writing his thesis on the history of architecture told me that in his first year he took a course in this field knowing little about it. It was a whole new venture for him, and the course had a strong positive impact. He began to look at his physical environment in new ways. He describes the way the professor began to reveal "how historians of architecture think":

> The professor presented examples of important buildings and small communities across different periods in history, and also across different cultures. Instead of just lecturing about various architectural styles, and naming and describing them, he assigned these facts as readings. And he set a precedent from the first week of assuming each of us in the class was always keeping up with the readings. He used precious class time to initiate a few extra steps. Those extra steps made a big difference.
>
> Each time we discussed the readings, he asked a question that related a particular building or community to a way of thinking. For example, he sometimes asked, "Why do you think this particular building is important? Is it mainly the details of the physical architecture? Or perhaps is it because the way this building is situated shapes the life of the city around it? How can a historian judge if a particular building or small neighborhood has played an important role in the development of a city's culture?" This professor encouraged debates among students, and occasionally expanded on a student's remark by saying, "Now that is how a historian might think about such a building, and here is why I say that."

Whenever he took that approach, a noticeable hush fell over the room. It was clear that all of us wanted to understand how he and his colleagues approach his work. That is what we really care about. And that is exactly what most textbooks don't convey too well.

I learned something really important from that class. I learned that time spent in classes where a professor simply goes over and repeats what I have just read, or could easily read in a textbook, is not the best use of time. And that time is so precious. What is most exciting is when a professor helps me to understand how people in his field think about topics in his field. I know this isn't always easy for a professor to do. Yet I wish every professor tried it. And it is critical he teach things in class that I couldn't really learn on my own, reading a textbook at the beach. Frankly, if I could do it on my own, then why should I be here? Especially at these prices.

## Encouraging Students to Disagree with the Professor

Building on earlier research by my colleagues David Pillemer and Sheldon White, we asked each senior we interviewed to identify a particular critical moment or unforgettable experience in their education. Every senior was able to do this, and 61 percent of them chose an experience that involved interacting with a faculty member around substantive academic work.

More than half of those seniors described a situation in which the academic task was for a student to take some significant responsibility in shaping the student-faculty interaction. In particular, students mention professors who encourage students to disagree—constructively—with what they are presenting. There is a delicate line between ceding all responsibility to a student and encouraging that student to take a reasonable amount of responsibility for shaping his own ideas and arguments. Faculty who are able to walk that line are remembered with honor by their students.

As one student made clear, encouraging disagreement from students can be part of teaching them how to think like professionals.

I didn't know quite what to do. I felt no matter what I said, I would be directly contradicting this distinguished professor's life's work. If I agreed with the remarks he just made, I would be disagreeing with the key assumptions and arguments in his book. If I cited his book in support of anything I said, it might seem that I hadn't been listening today.

I guess I wasn't the only one who felt uncomfortable. No one said anything. Finally the professor broke into a huge smile and said something like, "Good. It appears I have succeeded in presenting two different arguments, and you are having a hard time figuring out how to choose between them. That is what people in my field do all the time. So let's take the arguments one at a time, first the arguments from the book, then the arguments from class today, and let's see how a political scientist might think about them. Let's explore how a political theorist approaches such a problem."

Wow, did that man ever get our attention. Many of us had read pretty widely in political theory. We all could talk Rawls on justice and Nietzsche on the basic goodness, or lack of goodness, of human beings. But now for the first time I was putting on the shoes of a political theorist. And the fact that this professor is a very famous fellow, widely cited by others, didn't exactly hurt. But far more than his fame, what all of us in the seminar loved is the effort he made to help us learn how people in his field think.

I had been thinking about law school for the future, and I worried because I know some people choose law school without really knowing why they are doing it. In this political theory class, I learned a lot about myself. And it is because I learned to think like a political scientist. This professor suggested we might find it helpful to use a comparative approach to assess different political systems. And as the seminar unfolded I began to realize that differences in legal systems are a critical ingredient of how well different political systems function. I recall a couple of other professors had actually made that point in their classes. But they were talking *at* us. In this class I really figured it out for myself while the professor was helping me learn to "think like a political theorist."

Now I have begun thinking a lot for myself how different legal principles and structures shape different forms of democracy. It took that class and that teaching style to bring it all together. The only way I could really internalize the idea was by figuring it out for myself. I am now not only really enthusiastic about pursuing legal studies, I even have a dream for the future. Maybe one day I can help to write, or contribute to developing, a constitution for a country. I know it isn't likely to happen, but I do dream about it. All this work I'm doing really has a purpose. And it is clearly due to that seminar, and the professor's helping me to understand what it means to think like a political scientist. My life will always be changed now.

## Teaching the Use of Evidence

I am a statistician, so a large part of my research and teaching focuses on uses of evidence. A surprising number of undergraduates describe learning how to use evidence to resolve controversies in their field, whatever their field, as a breakthrough idea. Perhaps all of us on faculties need to realize that students may not know how to search for, gather, and interpret evidence to decide on what they believe, and to choose among alternatives in their field.

Nearly all the anecdotes students tell about learning to use systematic evidence involve courses they took in their first year. Students come to college with strong views on a variety of matters. Some of these views are political, others are social. Still others are intellectual in the sense that students hold a certain scientific perspective, or an opinion about good social policy, or even a perspective on what constitutes good literature or history or philosophy.

As students tell it, the question then is how to decide what they believe, across many disciplines, and what evidence to use in making such decisions. I am not referring here to the details of statistics, or econometrics, or decision analysis, or historiography. Of course those details are critical for students in those fields. Rather, I am referring to the way students develop and internalize a certain way of thinking. This evidence-based way of thinking is what helps undergraduates choose among alternatives, form a core philosophy, and transcend opinions they arrived with, even strongly held opinions.

The point is that students remember with special warmth faculty members who introduced them to ways of using evidence to make decisions and resolve controversies. And the sheer personal pleasure for faculty members who do this can be very high. One of the great virtues of working with undergraduates is that many of them feel free to question theories that we middle-aged faculty members rarely question because we are so used to them. Students point out that sometimes their questions actually get a faculty member to change his or her mind about a topic. For many students, at many colleges, constantly challenging professors is their greatest pleasure. Ideally they do it with great respect and civility. In any case, they do it. This offers professors a chance to teach students about the use of evidence.

Examples of this point abound; I present just one here. Students say they want as much of this as they can get. I take them at their word.

In a seminar on education policy, one first-year student repeatedly castigated the political leadership in her city and her state for not spending more money on public education. She brought this up several times. Once she brought it up in a discussion of declining measures of student performance. She held the reduced spending responsible. Most other members of that seminar agreed with her. Everyone spoke up. Everyone had an opinion.

The professor had an opinion too. Yet as this young woman tells it, he invited all the students to reserve judgment on this question until they had some concrete evidence. "What evidence," he asked, "could you gather in the real world, that would get you to change your minds?" The young woman reports that she couldn't think of a good answer. The professor asked a more specific question: "Would you find the results of a simple correlational study compelling, if you learned school districts that spend more have students who perform better on most academic measures?"

That question split the class in half. Half agreed they would find such results compelling. The other half demurred, pointing out that correlation does not necessarily imply causation. Maybe the reason students in richer districts do better in school is that they grow up in richer families, or have better-educated parents, or have more books at home and in their better-stocked school libraries. This class then engaged in a vigorous debate about the merits of observational, cross-sectional data for policy decisions, versus experimental data.

The young woman says that this discussion opened a whole new way of thinking for her. As a result, by the time of her interview she had taken four courses in statistics and research design and was planning to go to graduate school in public policy, with an emphasis on education policy. The professor in her first-year seminar, by getting the class to think hard about the role of evidence and what kinds of evidence would change their minds, changed the way she thought about making policy decisions:

Whether or not he intended it, that professor taught me soon after I arrived here that my good intentions about spending money on schools are very nice, but do not make for compelling public policy. His big message is that good intentions are a wonderful place to begin, but that when crunch time comes in the real world, evidence will trump good intentions every time. I had never thought of all my work in that way before that professor pressed me, and everyone else in our seminar, to think in those terms.

## Not Being Predictable

What happens in an ideal interaction between professor and student? The professor asks certain questions. He assigns a certain task. It may be a piece of writing, or a problem set, or a laboratory project. When the student works at the task, the professor gives detailed reactions to the work. Finally, he shares his own perspective on the task at hand. The way this last step is implemented points to a critical discriminator among professors.

The discriminator is that students overwhelmingly prefer to work with professors who are not too predictable. This is particularly true in the social sciences. Students honor predictability in faculty members' demands for excellent writing. They honor predictability in faculty members' standards for how to critique the work of philosophers, biologists, economists, psychologists, historians, or political theorists. But they emphatically do not honor predictability in the details of a faculty member's view of a bundle of dilemmas or controversies. Many students describe their disappointment when they meet a professor who, in the writer Anne Fadiman's words, "has chosen sides in the culture wars." As soon as students know how such a professor feels about one or two issues, they can predict with near perfect certainty how that professor will feel about dozens of other issues. And they find this predictability terribly disappointing. They say it suggests the professor isn't rigorously evaluating each issue independently, on its own merits. This is an idea faculty members may want to keep in mind as they choose readings and structure classroom discussions.

## Integrating Ideas from Other Disciplines

Many seniors single out interdisciplinary classes as the courses that meant the most to them. As a corollary, they cite faculty members who, while expert in their own fields, are able to put their fields in broader perspective. Students find this important. They believe that the real world, and the way people think about the world, does not divide neatly into categories called history, chemistry, literature, psychology, and politics.

Yet since colleges are organized around these disciplines, students feel they must constantly reorganize their thinking in a way that differs from the fundamental organization of the college. Students are entirely aware of the realities of organizing a college. They understand that some organizing mechanism is necessary. They understand the value of academic departments. They do not offer proposals to reorganize the current disciplinary structure. They simply observe that what serves as an important convenience to the institution sometimes makes it hard for them to get the big picture.

When students criticize the existing departmental structure, I ask what they would put in its place. Nearly all give the same answer. They describe the tension that many students feel between being specialists and being generalists. They are proud to be educated in depth in one or two fields, but this is not enough. They want more cross-cutting experiences.

When I told a group of colleagues what so many students were saying, they reminded me that enrollment in interdisciplinary honors programs on our campus (history and literature, history and science, social studies, folklore and mythology, and environmental policy studies), as on many others, has been rising steadily. They reminded me also that more and more students are pursuing double majors. So we concluded that students who say they want more interdisciplinary experiences are not simply offering an abstract wish list. Their actual behavior, course selections, and commitments for senior theses reflect what they say. And in regard to students' actual choices, particular faculty members can make a real difference.

How can students synthesize ideas and concepts across disciplines? The interviews identify three ways. One is to choose courses that are consciously designed to integrate. A second option is to try to do it on their own. That is clearly difficult, even for extraordinary students. A third way is for faculty members to facilitate the process. Students praise faculty members who go out of their way to create something of a multidisciplinary experience, even in a traditional class within a discipline. To do this, a professor often creates a task that draws on the different expertise and backgrounds of class members.

The format mentioned most often is when a professor poses a public policy problem and develops alternative solutions in the context of an academic discipline. Several students give the example of a professor of earth and planetary sciences who poses the problem to his class of how to reduce acid rain in the northeastern United States and Canada. The class begins by focusing on the science of acid rain. The professor then introduces what he calls "reality" into the discussion. That brings in a study of wind flows and climatology and atmospheric changes due to acid.

Just when the class feels they are getting a good handle on the science of controlling acid rain, the professor raises the question of political involvement. How can one country get this done? Students begin to think about trade-offs between clean air (they all support clean air), and jobs in factories for blue-collar workers who may have no easy alternatives (they all support jobs for such workers). And finally, in the last two sessions, the professor raises the international question—what can be done to facilitate cooperation between two countries, such as the United States and Canada? Especially when one country exports most of the acid rain and the economic consequences fall differentially on the two countries?

This is just one of many examples. I choose it because several students mentioned it as a particularly memorable example of a faculty member who built interdisciplinary ideas into a course taught within the traditional confines of a department. And I find it especially appealing because while building interdisciplinary challenges into disciplines such as government or economics or history does not seem too hard, this is an illustration from the sciences. My guess is that most undergraduates do not think of the department of earth and planetary sciences as a hotbed of synthesis across fields.

This example reminds us that students praise professors who helped them to think beyond traditional disciplinary boundaries. I view students' wish to bridge traditional departments as an opportunity for any faculty member in any department to be creative in teaching, and to make a profound difference in students' lives.

# 7

## DIVERSITY ON CAMPUS

When friends ask about the single biggest change over time I have observed on American campuses, the answer is simple. Anyone can see it in five minutes just by walking around. The change is in the students—who they are, how they look, and their backgrounds. This phenomenon is often called "the new student diversity." I prefer to think of it as students bringing different backgrounds to campus. These differences are racial, ethnic, political, geographical, and economic. Both inside and outside of classes, any student now, inevitably, mixes and mingles with a far more heterogeneous group of fellow students than I mixed with in college thirty-five years ago.

Back then, nearly all my fellow students were white. Most were men. Most came from middle-class backgrounds. This was true at Ivy League colleges, state universities, and small independent colleges. It was true throughout higher education, except for historically black institutions.

Now, slightly over half of students on most campuses are women, and nearly 25 percent of all undergraduates across America are nonwhite. Also, a significant fraction of students come from families of modest economic backgrounds. For example, one out of six Harvard undergraduates now comes from a family with an annual income of less than $20,000.

At Harvard in 1963, three men attended for every woman. Today the numbers are close to fifty-fifty. The Harvard class of 1963 had 17 nonwhite students—one percent of the class. The class of 2004, students here as I write this, includes about 600 nonwhite students, or more than 35 percent of the class. The campus looks different.

Today's students—white and nonwhite alike—know that at college they will be part of a diverse community, and they wonder how this new feature of American colleges will affect them. In this chapter and the next, I summarize what students have to say about this new heterogeneity.

## Access and Educational Impact

Students from all ethnic and racial backgrounds note that any discussion of diversity on campus should be separated into two parts. One part is the question of *access*. Do students from different backgrounds have, at the simplest level, the opportunity to attend a given college? The second part is the question of *educational impact*. What is the impact, educationally and personally, on students from all ethnic and racial backgrounds, of attending college with fellow students from diverse backgrounds?

These are separable questions. The second one is conditional, and depends upon the answer to the first. Nonwhite undergraduates are especially sensitive to this distinction. Many of them point out that historically the major challenge facing nonwhite students has been access. A few argue that even now the only critical issue is access. The handful of nonwhite undergraduates who make this point (five of the ninety nonwhite students I interviewed about race and ethnicity on campus) believe what really matters is that nonwhites get access to the same classes and professors and feedback and activities at college as whites. In their view, the educational impact on each student of having a diverse student body is a second-level question.

An overwhelming majority (the other eighty-five of those ninety students) disagree. They acknowledge that access is a prerequisite for everything else. Yet they believe the question of access has been pretty well resolved. They say that while access was denied in the past, this is no longer true. These students' main hope, now that they have a "seat at the table," is to participate fully in the conversation. That means learning, teaching, sharing, discussing, and questioning.

Every undergraduate I interviewed believes he or she has something unique and valuable to contribute to many conversations on campus. This conviction of having something to offer, along with an enthusiasm about interacting with students whose backgrounds differ from their own, is widespread among undergraduates from all ethnic and racial groups. And students say that the reason for making the original distinction, between simple access and diversity's educational impact, is that they see no value in fighting yesterday's battles. The access has been hard won, over a period of years, but it has indeed been won. So eighty-five of the ninety nonwhite undergraduates assert their wish to benefit from the diverse college community that now exists. Accomplishing this, these students say, requires opportunities for interactions both inside and outside of classrooms.

## An Ideal Environment

Students stress that certain environments facilitate learning from people with different backgrounds far more than others do. A college or university, and especially a selective one, should offer a particularly conducive environment.

Why do students believe this? Because, they say, regardless of any individual's background, nearly all students arrive on campus with certain goals, expectations, and aspirations. Most first-year students who have given this topic some thought understand that at college they will meet others with different ideas and from different economic, geographical, religious, and ethnic and racial backgrounds. These differences may be substantial. For some students they may be jarring.

At the same time, first-year students arriving at a college, especially a selective college, also know that the fellow students they meet will be like them in certain ways. They will have worked hard, usually very hard, in high school. They will intend to continue to work hard at college. Students expect to meet people who will disagree with them. Indeed, they look forward to meeting such people. As part of this mix, they know they will meet people from different ethnic and racial groups.

Advocates of the benefits of racial and ethnic diversity argue that, almost inevitably, good consequences flow when people get to know others from different backgrounds. Our students find the reality of getting to know others from different backgrounds far more complex. As a young man from Chicago says, "Anyone can do that by just walking on the streets of a major city."

The crux of students' observations about learning from people with different backgrounds is that college offers a fundamentally different opportunity from most other environments. The opportunity arises precisely because all incoming students are likely to share certain values. Each student assumes that all other students, whatever their background, understand this and will behave accordingly. One such shared value is that students will learn not just from professors but also from their experiences with one another. Living together. Preparing for classes together. Arguing in classes together. Working together. Playing together.

Students point out that how well ethnic and racial diversity actually enhances learning depends largely on how well a college builds on, capitalizes on, and proactively strengthens this basic assumption. They say that if this assumption of certain shared values is undercut by campus culture, or faculty members, or college leadership, or even the leaders of student organizations, then positive educational benefits may not flow from diversity of ethnic and racial backgrounds. The risk is that awkwardness may destroy learning.

I stress this point because students feel particularly strongly about it. A large number note that these four years at college may be one of the few opportunities of a lifetime to live in an environment in which nearly all members of the community really do share a critical set of assumptions. Assumptions about hard work, academic rigor, excellence, and taking commitments to classes as well as to outside-of-class activities seriously.

Certain organizations, and a selective college is one, are particularly likely to offer an environment in which such key assumptions are widely shared. In such an environment, it is natural and comfortable and quite ordinary for any members of that community to talk with, mix and mingle with, and learn something from people whose backgrounds differ from their own. Student after student asserts that when the campus atmosphere encourages such assumptions, the diversity on campus leads to several kinds of learning from those who are ethnically or racially different. For many students on many campuses, especially those who grew up in relatively homogeneous communities, this kind of learning is new.

An African-American junior stressed the importance of atmosphere or tone:

> I just can't say enough about the importance of setting a tone of good will. And this is where my first year proctor (residence hall advisor) was a big-time success from the very beginning.
>
> In my case, the proctor had us all in her living room in the first week. There were about twenty of us, of varying backgrounds and races. I remember it so well because after some friendly introductions she looked right at me and asked with a smile, "Do you prefer to be called African American or black?" I certainly did not anticipate such a question, but responded by simply saying, "African American." Then the proctor asked, "Would you feel offended if another student, not knowing your preference, referred to you as black?" Of course I told her I wouldn't be offended at all. How could a stranger possibly know my preference?
>
> Then she turned to a Latina woman and asked about being called Latina as opposed to Hispanic. She moved on to ask a Chinese American, born here in the states, how he would feel if another student referred to him simply as an "Asian." She even asked a white guy whether he preferred white or Caucasian. And each time after she got an answer, she followed up by asking whether we would be offended if someone used the other, less preferred word. Would we assume that new person was a racist, or thoughtless, because of how they referred to us?
>
> It took us a while to catch on, but soon it became ob-

vious the proctor was just conveying a simple idea. She was demonstrating by her own behavior that she didn't know what each of us prefers to be called, but that she hopes we will assume she means well. And that it follows we will also assume other students on campus mean well when they do the same thing.

I think she did something very important. She got us all to think how we would react to different ethnic or racial descriptors. Her point is that each of us must choose. And much of our next four years would depend on the choice we make. We can each choose to assume good will from all other students, or we can bring in all the hostilities and awkwardnesses from the outside world.

I am really glad this happened during the first week. It reminded me about assuming good will among my fellow students, and I think others felt the same way. In fact, I am certain they did, since eight of us still live together three years later. We must be the most multiracial group around. For example, the four of us in my rooming group happen to include a Christian, a Jew, a Muslim, and a Hindu. Try that on for size.

For this tone to take root, students must arrive with a certain perspective. And campus leaders at all levels must reinforce it. The perspective is not liberal or conservative. It is just an openmindedness. It is an eagerness to meet and engage with people who look different from oneself and come from different backgrounds. The big point is that this variation in backgrounds will often lead to different conversations, different questions, and different debates from what would come up in an all-white, all-black, all-Asian, all-Latino, or all-anything community. Students believe this perspective—this "tone of good will"—is a prerequisite that any college must put into place so students can quickly get beyond the trivialities of "how different we look," and begin to interact and to learn from one another.

## Negative Diversity in High Schools

When students talk about diversity in their high schools, they do not paint a pretty picture. Their characterizations of high school interactions do not support the argument that simply exposing people to others who are different will inevitably lead to constructive learning and improved relationships. Students describe a sharply different situation.

Diversity in high school, at least as reported by Harvard undergraduates, is not working well at all. First, the numbers. Of the 120 undergraduates with whom I explored this question directly, 44 reported little or no ethnic diversity in their high schools. So for this group, "how well it is working" was a moot point.

For the other 76 undergraduates, a clear pattern emerged. Of the 22 who attended private or independent high schools, 19 ranked their personal experience with fellow students from ethnic groups other than their own as either "positive" or "highly positive." The 54 students who attended public high schools presented a very different picture: 38, or more than two-thirds, characterized their personal experience as "negative" and "disappointing." Each was invited to give specific reasons. While the details differ, a broad conclusion quickly becomes clear. The conclusion is that American public schools, at least those attended by the undergraduates I interviewed, make remarkably little effort to build a sense of community or shared culture. This is in sharp contrast to reports from graduates of independent schools.

The two-thirds of undergraduates from public high schools who characterized their high school experience with diversity as "disappointing" had little hesitation in explaining why. They said that the leaders of their schools made little or no effort to encourage the development of shared values among students from different backgrounds. Students in their high schools arrived with and then continued to bring to school each day many of the biases, preconceptions, and values of their families and communities. Then they simply replicated these values and behaviors each day at school.

A South Asian–American student told me what he called an awkward story from his own life:

All through high school I faced a dilemma created by the diversity within my school. It illustrates how even a strong community can be shattered by members of one group who are insensitive to how members of another group think or feel. And especially when leaders of different groups in a community truly differ in what they value and reward. Maybe what happened to me will be helpful for other people to know.

Here I am—obviously a person of color. Both of my parents immigrated here from India. My skin is quite dark, and I have always been struck by the expression "persons of color." It obviously includes me. Just look at me. I never imagined the heartache such a categorization would create.

In my high school, near Chicago, the student body is about 30 percent people of color. It is actually a nice mix of just about every ethnic group you can imagine.

I was a good student. I took the work very seriously, I worked hard. I was especially proud that besides taking several A.P. classes, I played on two varsity sports teams. Some of my closest friends, from all races, were classmates in my A.P. classes, and others were my teammates in sports. It was great for both freshman and sophomore year. No problems connected to race.

Then a disaster hit the school. Several parents of "students of color" decided at the end of my sophomore year they would sponsor an annual party. That's great, except it was going to also include an awards ceremony. And awards for various things would only be given to members of the Multicultural Students Association.

I suppose the parents who hatched this idea meant well. Maybe they felt students of color weren't winning enough awards at the regular school ceremonies. Our school had various prizes such as "best essay submitted by a sophomore" or "best debater in history class during junior year." In any event, I felt definitely uneasy about any subgroup of parents, by race, having a gathering to give out awards for which only students of color would be eligible. My first thought was, "What are they trying to accomplish by doing this—choosing a student and designating him or her as the "best debater of color"? I felt it was demeaning to me and all other students of color. It was exactly the opposite of "building a sense of community among people with differences."

Well, if I was uneasy, my mother became angry as hell. She said she would have nothing to do with it. The idea of giving awards and prizes by ethnic subgroup cut against everything she had raised me to believe in. Despite an idealized world where people are judged as individuals, this idea was going to classify people by race. Only people of certain races could win a prize. My mother wondered, what would happen if a

group of white parents decided to hold an awards ceremony for whites only?

But now picture my dilemma. Thanks to those parents' harebrained idea, I and many of my friends were
put in an impossible position. My friends of color, including some on the varsity sports teams, split into two
groups, and the groups got pretty angry with one another. At one point they weren't even talking. One
group thought it was a nice idea. The other agreed with
me, that you don't divide up the school into ethnic subgroups, almost like a kind of apartheid, and give separate prizes within each subgroup.

My many white friends also fell into two categories.
The majority just laughed it off as sad and pathetic. Several of them felt as offended as I did. Excellence and accomplishment, in their view, is what it is, regardless of
ethnic background.

Unfortunately, it gets even sadder. This idea came
from a small group of parents. And they defined "people
of color" as everyone who is nonwhite. That, of course,
includes me. As well as all African-Americans,
Asian-Americans, and the Latino students in the school.
Well, as events developed, I and my mother weren't the
only people of color who didn't want to come near this.
Most of the Asian students, and all the other Indian students, felt exactly the same way.

After a few weeks it became obvious these few parents had created, however unintentionally, the ultimate
irony. The strongest antagonisms that emerged were
clearly among subgroups of "people of color." When
many Asian and Indian students said they wouldn't
come to such an event, two African-American parents

accused them of racism. Look at me. Look at my skin. How do you think I felt, being accused of racism? How does someone ever fully recover from such an accusation?

You asked me whether I had had experiences in high school that led me to think about the diversity here at college. Well, I think the lesson for me from that situation is so strong that I will treasure the diversity here extra much. And I encourage all my fellow students of color to work hard to keep our time here a common experience for all of us. I think it is possible because we all have common values. We work hard and strive to do really good work. And I think we are mostly open-minded. Heaven forbid I ever have to repeat that high school experience in any way.

This young man's story illustrates that students from different ethnic groups often really do bring dramatically different sets of values to day-to-day classes in high school. Will it surprise any reader that Asian-American students report that in high school they and their fellow Asian-American students spent significantly more hours each week doing homework than students from other ethnic groups? Will it surprise any reader that white, Anglo students, especially those who are academically serious and ambitious, resent the impact on their learning, and on class discussions, of having students in their classes who barely speak and understand English?

These two examples were the ones brought up most often by students I interviewed. My interviewees felt they themselves were full of good will. Yet at the same time they were observing a reality. A reality that is particularly prevalent in urban schools. The reality is that when any student's serious commitment to education becomes compromised by certain types of accommodations to racial and ethnic diversity, that student's enthusiasm for diversity at school quickly erodes. Differences then create conflict instead of offering opportunities for learning. They reinforce each individual's worst stereotypes rather than breaking them down from personal observation. Of all the topics addressed in the interviews, students' reports about their experiences with diversity in high school stand alone in their negative tone.

These sharp differences between high school and college lead many students to conclude that while abstract observations about the benefits of diversity may sound uplifting, reality often trumps the abstractions. A large number make the point that certain preconditions must be put into place for diversity to enhance learning, at any college, inside or outside of classes.

Students believe their experiences at college are so different from high school for a critical reason, a reason I have already mentioned. It is that at college, especially at a selective college, all of their fellow undergraduates, regardless of ethnic background, or geography, or political perspective, or financial circumstance, share certain core values. The result is that each member of the college community can make certain assumptions about all other members of the community. Each assumes other students are here because they treasure the value of a good education. Worked hard to get here. Expect to have their thinking challenged in class. Expect to contribute in class. A graduating senior, a white woman, told me this story about her high school experience:

I think any discussion using the word "diversity," especially when it comes to its educational value, must take place in a context. When I came to college, I had had some pretty bad experiences with the so-called benefits of diversity. So it wasn't obvious to me what the big benefits are.

In ninth grade, in my public school in New York, we had an influx of Latino immigrants. They were my age, and they either didn't speak English at all, or if they did it was pretty marginal. There were about six of these folks in my classrooms of about 26. The classes in history and social studies truly fell to pieces. The teacher was good, and tried hard. But how would you like to teach history in a class where one-quarter of the students understand neither what you are saying nor what is generally going on?

It degenerated pretty quickly. It became destructive chaos. All of the serious students felt incredibly angry that our education was going down the drain. Everything really hit the fan when we had a class debate on rent control in the context of studying the Supreme Court. I really care about that. I was one of the debaters. I prepared hard for days. So did several of my friends.

During the debate, first the kids who didn't speak English started fidgeting. Then they stopped pretending to listen. Then they started talking among themselves. Then they started laughing. They ended up disrupting the whole thing. I was practically in tears. And I wasn't the only one. No education was taking place. This continued for weeks, despite the whole situation being an obvious disaster. Finally, my parents, who are deeply committed to the public schools, pulled me out and sent me to an independent school.

The irony is that there was actually more racial diversity among the kids in that independent school, and it worked pretty well.

I learned a big lesson. At my new school, the kids may have come from different ethnic groups and races, but we all shared an important assumption about why we all were there. And the school reinforced it by demanding a lot, and not tolerating any disruptions or fooling around.

The lesson is that it is mindless to simply assert that diversity among students inevitably leads to educational benefits. I have lived through the opposite, and it was awful. Any potential benefits depend heavily on the context, the setting, and most of all, whether there is enough of a fundamental set of shared skills and values to make it possible for us to learn from one another. Heaven knows I have nothing against immigrant kids. But to say that I benefited either academically or socially from their arrival in the classroom, with the language barrier and other problems, including disruptive behavior at school, would be a lie. So I came to college a bit leery of the much-vaunted diversity.

As you can guess, it is all different here. In fact two of my closest friends and living group members are Latina. I enjoy them and learn a lot from them. But the reason I can do that is that we share certain values and skills. It is those skills and those values that brought us all to college here in the first place. Diversity can be great when the context is right. But without at least a minimal sharing of fundamental values and skills, the educational value of student diversity may well be negative.

I think it is the responsibility of campus leaders, as well as those who decide who gets to come, to make sure we don't just see the downside of diversity. I saw it every day in high school, and it is exactly what I believe any good college can and should avoid. It does us, the students, no favor. If it were to happen here it would be unforgivable. After all, to use my favorite expression from economics classes, this is a controllable variable.

One point about diversity in high schools is brought up primarily by nonwhite students. It is that many high schools currently send a corrosive message to all students: the message that educational excellence is threatened when a school serves a racially or ethnically diverse group of students. As a result, "making racial and ethnic diversity work" is seen as an oppositional concept to demanding hard work to achieve excellence. Nonwhite undergraduates in particular report a troubling range of experiences in schools where "making it possible for students from different backgrounds to just get along" became the primary objective.

They believe this has catastrophic consequences. Rather than challenging students academically with the most rigorous educational program they can handle, leaders of some high schools are attempting to homogenize the experiences of all students. One result is that some white students and their parents resent it. Another result is that nonwhite students are, just like white students, not pushed to excel.

So in the eyes of some nonwhite undergraduates, they take a double hit. First, they are blamed by white students for weakening the quality of those students' education. And second, they themselves are not challenged. Instead, all members of the school community tacitly accept the unfortunate proposition that in order for everyone to "get along," rigor and excellence must be sacrificed. Nonwhite students in particular criticize this trade-off as unnecessary and carrying a heavy price. The price is that resentment flares across ethnic groups and it is hard for any individual to transcend these group tensions.

The policy prescription offered by these undergraduates is for leaders of American high schools to abandon this tendency to sacrifice the pursuit of excellence just so people can "get along." They find it ironic that such efforts, which were probably all well-intentioned at the outset, have led to both poorer academic experiences and inter-ethnic hostility. They also point out that it is mostly the nonwhite students, especially those from lower-income backgrounds, who suffer the biggest loss of opportunity on both dimensions—educational and personal.

## Diversity at College

Undergraduates differentiate between two types of learning. One is academic learning, in which academic topics and perspectives and ways of thinking are the focus of student interactions. The other is interpersonal learning. Here student interactions are built around learning about, and from, one another's different backgrounds and perspectives about life as well as school.

Responses to questions about the impact of diversity are sharp, clear, and overwhelmingly positive. One Latina student told interviewer Shu-Ling Chen:

> Learning from diversity depends so much on being a reflective student. I feel like for the first eighteen years of my life there has been a veil. Coming to college has taken off that veil. It takes your ideals and forces you to look back and reconsider them. That's how this education affects my life. It affects how I treat people and

how I think about my relationship with those people. I learn a lot from this real-world experience.

White students are the most positive about how fellow undergraduates from other races and ethnic groups have taught them much they would not have learned or even thought of otherwise. They are closely followed in a three-way tie by Asian-American, Latino, and African-American students. When I pressed the 120 students I interviewed on this topic for examples of something they had learned because of the diversity among undergraduates, only 9 students were unable to think of such an example. The other 111 found it pretty easy.

About 20 percent of the specific examples came from classroom discussions. Many students mention situations in which, in a small class or seminar, a person whose ethnic background is different from their own interprets an idea or a written work or a historical document in a way they did not expect. Often students recall fellow students making arguments that clearly flowed from different assumptions or different starting points, and there is a clear correlation between these unexpected arguments and different ethnic backgrounds. While not all professors seem able to capitalize on such educational moments, many do well at it, and this is when maximum learning takes place.

The other 80 percent of the examples come from events or interactions or conversations outside of classes. They may be from a discussion in a residence hall, or over a meal, or at a rehearsal for a dramatic production or a singing or dance performance.

I took a class on Jerusalem, which dealt with biblical archaeology. As a Muslim, this was my first encounter with reading the Bible and learning about the view of

Christianity and Judaism. A friend of mine who was taking the class is Christian. I asked him a lot of questions about the early stories of Jesus. He also described how his brother was baptized in Bethlehem. These conversations, mostly outside of class but initiated by class discussions and the assigned readings, helped me to understand why the course material we were studying is significant.

They helped me to understand the personal and emotional connections that people attribute to these sites, which can be very different from the "objective" and sometimes sterile academic view that textbooks and even lectures can present. So they gave me a context in which to make sense of what I was learning.

A large number of students mention situations in which students from different ethnic and racial backgrounds work together to arrange and supervise an event. This may involve arranging a speakers' series on campus co-sponsored by students from different ethnic groups. It may involve arranging public debates on politically controversial topics. The very process of planning such a debate offers a great opportunity for undergraduates to engage with one another on topics about which they may disagree, while they are simultaneously working together to make a public debate work well and to make a positive contribution to the entire campus community. A Latina senior talked about such a situation:

I think one of the reasons our Forums are so well attended and so successful is that we always try to get several co-sponsors together for each event. I am not exactly sure how that started historically, but I heard that

147

a few years ago a couple of student groups, working entirely alone, invited speakers whose sole redeeming value seemed to be their capacity to preach anger and even hatred of other ethnic groups.

Understandably, that enraged different groups. Things got pretty tense, apparently. I can hardly believe those stories, they are so offensive. If I thought that some other ethnic organization had specifically chosen to invite a speaker whose main focus is preaching contempt for other groups, I would be pretty outraged too. What are we here, ten years old?

Apparently after that happened, two deans and the president held a series of meetings among student leaders to try to change the way such events are developed and organized. They sure seem to have succeeded. In my few years here, nearly every night there are speakers who arrive here with a joint invitation from blacks and whites, Latinos and Asians.

We have a Latin American policy series that is co-sponsored by about six groups, two of which are Latino, yet the groups include both Democrats and Republicans as well as different ethnic groups. And of course Cultural Rhythms is pretty much everyone's favorite activity—it features snippets of many different cultures, and it seems like just about every ethnic group on campus is sponsoring it. It really is a healthy atmosphere. Maybe it is a virtuous circle.

## MEANINGS OF DIVERSITY

One finding that I did not expect is the emphasis some students, especially nonwhite students, put on the word "diversity" as conveying disagreements within their own ethnic or racial community. These students stressed that for them these disagreements are yet another source of learning and personal maturation. They note that a great strength of studying in a college with a substantial number of members of their own racial group is that they can learn from disagreements with their fellow students.

One graduating senior, an African American, told me about a class he took. He asked that if I chose to share his example I should characterize it as his "journey of discovery."

I will guess that most people you interview tell you how diversity on campus, for them, means interacting with students from different backgrounds. In my case, the learning from diversity came in an entirely different way. It has little to do with whites or Latinos or Asians. It happened when I became very upset about how a fellow black student approached discussions in our sociology class.

The topic of the class was, roughly speaking, "Who gets ahead in America?" We studied works by Jencks and Riesman, and as sociology concentrators we all had pretty good backgrounds in statistics. So I was eager to read some pretty controversial texts, including *The Bell Curve* and *The Shape of the River*. As you know, these two books put forth very different perspectives on the role of race in understanding who gets ahead in America. I did not expect to agree with much in *The Bell Curve*, but I was eager to read it, and fully prepared that what I read might upset me.

Well, I was far more surprised by our class discussion than by any analyses in these two books. One day in class we were discussing illegitimate birth rates, broken down by race. The professor rather matter-of-factly presented birth rates for several ethnic groups. Those data included the fact that for blacks the illegitimate birth rate has hovered around 70 percent for the past ten years. I was stunned when one of my black classmates became visibly angry and accused the professor of not realizing how much it hurt him to hear such information presented in class. Thank goodness he did it politely and not accusingly. But he was obviously upset. And his upset got me very upset, but in the opposite direction.

This was the whole reason I had signed up to take this course. I need to grapple with unpleasant realities. I can't imagine that ignoring them helps anyone. I hope to help my community in future work. Yet it seems kind of obvious to me that the first step in improving any situation is facing the facts squarely, even when they are awkward and uncomfortable. Then, once we recognize a problem, we can try to think of ways to improve the situation. And work our butts off to do so. But my fellow black student really made it awkward—both for the professor and for me. I actually wanted to hear more details about those demographics. Not because I am happy about them, but because I absolutely need to understand them as well as I can. Illusions are definitely no help.

Well, frankly, I didn't know quite what to do. My fellow student was simply shooting the messenger. The professor seemed as taken aback as I was. Thank goodness there was a third African-American student in the class. He had the courage to speak right up, and to thank the professor for sharing this awkward but real data. This guy basically said what I was thinking, except I didn't have the courage to verbalize it out loud.

The student who had complained to the professor seemed surprised that a fellow black student would criticize him. But this other student was so diplomatic that

I think he somehow succeeded in getting the complainer to take a deep breath and to pause and reconsider his views. It took some courage for that black student to criticize another black student who clearly was upset. And in the context of a mostly white class.

I think a lot of learning took place in that seminar. First, the fellow who was offended by hearing the real-world data quickly learned that two other black students not only weren't offended, they felt exactly the opposite. They wanted more discussion of this unpleasant topic, not less. I think that led him to at least reconsider his assumptions.

Second, all the other students saw for themselves that there is some diversity of perspectives among the black students here. I think that is a good thing. Especially because it is really true. And of course it isn't only true among black students—it is true among all subsets of students from all backgrounds.

I guess you could say that a truly awkward moment became a positive learning experience for most of the class. I learned something from that exchange. The two other black students learned something. And I'm pretty sure most of the white students learned something important just watching our brief exchange of comments. For me, as an African-American guy, this idea of learning from disagreement within a group is one benefit of the word "diversity" that too often gets overlooked.

## Bringing Different Perspectives to College

If, on average, students who are African American, Asian American, Latino, and white all arrived on campus having read the same books, with the same distribution of political perspectives, with the same distribution of future hopes and dreams, and with the same distribution of perspectives on history—then it would be hard to argue that racial and ethnic diversity enhanced the academic component of a college education. Perhaps personal relationships across groups would be enhanced, but it would take some differences among groups in an academic sense to invigorate classroom learning.

Students from different subgroups actually do bring several such differences. Students' backgrounds often result in their exposure to different literature, different perspectives about societal institutions such as police protection and crime control, and different expectations about how the leadership of a college or university will treat them. These differences challenge everyone on campus to respond constructively. As long as students interact across groups both in classes and in situations of living, working, studying, and socializing, they can learn something different, something more, than what they would learn on a campus without those racial and ethnic differences.

## RECOMMENDED READING

We asked students what books "of the modern era" they considered "especially important." What writers did they believe their fellow students should read? Several differences among subgroups were apparent.

A sharp difference emerged between men and women, regardless of ethnicity. Approximately one-third of all women named Betty Friedan's *The Feminine Mystique* as a work they considered especially important. They described it as critical for understanding modern American cultural and social history. Not a single man mentioned this book. At least five women mentioned the following authors: Virginia

Woolf, Jane Austen, Doris Lessing, and Eudora Welty. None of these four authors was mentioned by more than one man. Two were not mentioned by any man.

Many African-American students mentioned books by Alice Walker and Nathan McCall. Not a single student who was not African American, zero out of ninety students, mentioned either of these two authors.

About one-quarter of Jewish students brought up various stories by Isaac Bashevis Singer. Not a single non-Jewish student mentioned any of Singer's works as especially important.

Several Muslim students named Naguib Mahfouz as the most important writer of modern times. Not a single non-Muslim student mentioned this writer. Since I had not read Mahfouz, I asked for details. I learned that Mahfouz was born in Cairo in 1911, and that he had written about thirty novels about the human condition and had won the 1988 Nobel Prize for Literature. One student told me, animatedly, that his favorite Mahfouz novel was *The Palace of Desire.* He said that Mahfouz had been influenced by writers as different as Flaubert, Balzac, Zola, Camus, Tolstoy, Dostoyevsky, and especially Proust. Another student chose *The Beginning and the End* as his favorite. Another praised *The Beggar.* I asked these students if they shared their insights and opinions with other students. They said yes, if the opportunity was right. Certainly they shared these observations in small groups, such as classroom seminars and with roommates and friends from all backgrounds.

Several Asian-American students brought up the work of Lu Hsun as especially important to them. Again I pressed, since I was not familiar with this writer. Students told me Lu Hsun was born in 1881 in China. Since he could not make a living as a writer, he spent many years as a university teacher. He wrote many short stories. One student identified "A Madman's Diary" as her favorite. Another mentioned "Village Opera." A third described "Medicine" in detail. When a fourth Asian-American student told me her favorite author was Lu Xun and she especially liked his story "The Flight to the Moon," I commented that she was the only person who had mentioned the author Lu Xun. "Did other students mention certain authors?" she asked. Yes, I told her, and shared with her the several responses identifying Lu Hsun. After a short pause, this young student blurted out, "Professor Light, this is the same man!" Not a single student other than Asian Americans mentioned this author.

The second most frequently mentioned author by Asian-American students was Shi Zhicun. When I asked one young man whether he ever shared his observations and insights with others, he mentioned bringing Shi Zhicun's writings into discussions in his psychology classes and history and literature classes. He said that Shi Zhicun's work transcends Asian culture and the realities of twentieth-century China and focuses more broadly on individual psychology. He told me that the work of fiction "One Evening in the Rainy Season" led to Shi Zhicun's organizing and editing a monthly literary magazine called *Les Contemporains.* I learned much from this discussion about how literary journals are started and managed, often by expatriates. This is precisely the kind of learning that takes place when two people from different backgrounds interact, and this time I was the beneficiary.

Latino students presented two authors as especially important. Several described Jorge Luis Borges of Argentina as the man who shaped the Latin American novel. One mentioned *Dr. Brodie's Report* as her favorite. A second chose *The Book of Sand.* A third chose *The Book of Imaginary Be-*

ings. Other students brought up the Mexican novelist Carlos Fuentes. One student talked about how his work *The Good Conscience* changed the way she thinks about human relationships. Another student brought up the works *Diana* and *Aura.* A third named the collection *Terra Nostra* as a leading work of Western literature. He described discussions and disagreements he had in several literature classes, and as a writer for two student publications, with Anglo students who were unfamiliar with Fuentes's works. He noted that while he often did not get other students to agree with him, at least he got them to read and discuss Fuentes's writings.

What do these examples illustrate? I believe they offer compelling evidence that students from different backgrounds indeed bring different tastes and preferences to the campus table. I should stress that, of course, substantial overlap in literary tastes exists as well. But the key point is that in interactions among students, certain different tastes that seem to reflect different ethnic backgrounds (or genders) are one way that students educate and learn from one another.

I do not believe that, to prove the educational benefits of diversity, Jewish students must begin to identify Nizar Qabbani as critically important to them. Nor must Muslim students identify Isaac Bashevis Singer. Nor must every college graduate become an expert on the works of Lu Hsun or Gabriel Garcia Marquez. But the backgrounds that students bring to college expand the possibilities. The critical ingredient is that interactions take place—in classes, or residence halls, or other settings—to enable students to talk about these authors and why they have such a profound impact. Students report that such interactions do occur more than occasionally. Yet they could profitably occur even more often.

Several students mentioned this particular example of "important authors" as a topic around which, on any campus, student leaders from different racial and ethnic groups might co-sponsor events. At such events, discussions about various authors' work can develop constructively and comfortably, and learning can mix with genuine pleasure. No one is testing anyone else or enforcing right or wrong answers—just sharing perspectives.

## EXPECTING THE COLLEGE TO CHANGE

A second finding that differentiates among ethnic groups is attitudinal. On average, students from different groups come to college with sharp disagreements about what they expect from the college as an institution. They differ on whether, and how, they expect the college to change because of their very presence. They differ on how to present their views to the leadership of the college. They differ on what aspects of college life—curriculum, advising, living arrangements, even their own course choices—should depend upon their ethnicity.

These disagreements lead to vigorous discussions on campus. Sometimes they lead to tensions among leaders of different ethnic group organizations, and sometimes they lead to tensions between student leaders and university leaders. While the discussions can be difficult, students from all backgrounds report that much learning, and often a significant changing of minds, takes place.

Asian-American students, overwhelmingly, feel it is not the obligation of a college to "change things" in response to their arrival. They feel this even though they, the Asian Americans, are a relatively new and increasingly prominent force on campus. Student after student expresses feeling privileged to have the opportunity to attend a particular college. Most describe feeling they are welcome guests at their new institution. They say directly that they chose freely to come to the college, and that as a consequence they believe they should accept most existing institutional structures. Most do not expect the college to restructure its course offerings, living arrangements, requirements, and support systems to accommodate them because they are a relatively new minority group on campus.

Both Latinos and African Americans have noticeably different perspectives. A solid majority believe that, as they are new groups on campus, the college should make some changes, sometimes major changes, to accommodate and welcome them. There is substantial disagreement about the details of what changes would be most constructive. The suggestion mentioned most frequently is more inclusion throughout the curriculum of readings by Latino and African-American authors. The second most frequent suggestion is a physical place on campus for members of these ethnic groups to gather, to socialize, to sponsor both academic and social events.

Whenever a student expressed a wish for a physical gathering place on campus, the interviewer followed up with a question about the desirability of separate, ethnically based dormitories or residence halls. Three students out of 120 who were asked this question said they thought such residences would be a good idea. Six others saw a mix of pluses and minuses. The other 111 were strongly opposed. They seemed to take pleasure in observing that we were asking them to tell in detail about their experiences, both the pluses and the minuses, of living with a diverse group of fellow students. Some said it was not clear to them how they would even be able to answer such a question if residence halls were organized by race or ethnicity. Feelings run strong on this point.

Among the many students interviewed during this project, those from Latino backgrounds were particularly mixed in their views about "special treatment" of any kind. Responses from these students were split almost exactly fifty-fifty on questions of how much a college should change to accommodate them. And those who opposed excessive categorizing of any student by ethnic group offered striking illustrations from their own years at college.

Anna Fincke, a student interviewer, found that even when nonwhite students get "special treatment" because an institution makes special efforts because of ethnic factors, it often turns out to be a mixed blessing. Especially in the eyes of those students. In real-life situations, such special treatment often leads to awkwardness for nonwhite students, and a sense of being patronized. Fincke reports an example from a Latina woman:

> I went to the Career Fair last week. There was a booth there with a woman who was with an organization which was seeking educators of color for New England independent schools. I walked over and a woman who was obviously Hispanic was there talking to the woman at the booth. She walked away and I walked up and asked, "What's this about?" The woman looks at me from head to toe and gives me a pamphlet and says, "Why don't you call this number." And I stood there expecting her to tell me more but she didn't.
>
> So I asked again and she pointed to the number again. So I said, "I'll call the number, but what are you doing here?" She said, "We're looking to diversify the teaching staffs of independent schools across New England." I

asked what she meant by diversify and she spoke in terms of color. I asked what she meant by color and she said "nonwhite." Then she asked what I considered myself and I said, "Sometimes white, sometimes not." And I explained both my parents were born in Cuba. She lit up and said, "You're Hispanic! I couldn't tell!" She got all excited and started speaking to me in Spanish and saying, "You're just the type of person we are looking for." She had me filling out papers, taking home brochures. I thought it was funny and sad.

As for white students, they are thoroughly mixed in their views about how this college, or any college, should adjust to welcome new groups of students. About 60 percent of white students support, often quite strongly, the principle that new courses should be offered, and existing courses should be modified, to accommodate and support such groups. The other 40 percent disagree, often strongly. Their perspective is that the college has certain traditions, and that while gradual change is both good and inevitable, such change should reflect new and exciting substantive areas of work in academic disciplines, not ethnic changes on campus. Several students mentioned the two new interdisciplinary concentrations—Environmental Policy and Mind, Brain, and Behavior—as examples of highly positive curriculum change. Each campus will have its own set of institutions that students may accept or challenge. It is important to shape the conversation that accompanies any such challenge so that it becomes a constructive learning experience, not a simple fight for authority.

# 8

## LEARNING FROM DIFFERENCES

The topic of ethnic and racial diversity is a highly charged political issue on many campuses. Therefore, students may want to think about how they will approach this issue in their years at college. If their parents attended an American college or university, the modern version will probably be noticeably different. Not just in terms of course coverage, but perhaps most of all in terms of campus atmosphere. What can any student from any background learn from the experience of studying and living and working on campus in this new atmosphere? In this chapter I present several findings, all from students, that suggest how attending college with others from varied backgrounds can influence and enhance both learning and personal life. Students describe their experiences studying, living, learning, working, and playing on a diverse campus.

One key theme is that diversity on campus exerts an impact on learning both in and out of classes. A second theme is that interactions among students often have powerful effects on people from many different backgrounds—not just any one subgroup. A third theme is that while many interactions are positive, some are clearly the opposite. About two-thirds of the examples students give are strikingly positive. Some tell about discussions with fellow students from different racial and ethnic groups that enhance academic learning. Others describe a process of interpersonal growth. Yet several tell of troubling encounters.

Several of the findings are unexpected, at least to me. I did not expect so many students to respond to questions about the educational impact of diversity by describing complex incidents that led simultaneously to academic and personal growth. I did not expect students to identify so many incidents that occur outside of classes, often in residence halls, as the ones they remember most vividly. And I had no idea of the importance of religious life and religious diversity for many undergraduates. Student after student characterizes religious diversity as an especially powerful source of learning. Let us begin with that finding.

## Religious Diversity as a Positive Force

When I ask students about the impact of diversity, many bring some aspect of religious diversity into their response. At the outset I focused primarily on racial and ethnic diversity. But I quickly learned that these are intertwined with religion. Understanding the power of students' religious convictions offers some insight into the impact of ethnic diversity.

Religious diversity plays a role in classroom discussions and debates that can serve a powerful educational function. This is most likely to happen when students are able to integrate their religious perspectives into their classes and express them directly. Faculty members who are comfortable inviting and dealing with such comments can capitalize on them to enhance classroom discussion. And students who feel comfortable integrating a spiritual aspect of their life with what may sometimes seem like abstract academic concepts may find that this combination leads to powerful learning.

Why are students so convinced of the educational value

of religious diversity? Some report being surprised, taken aback, or even shocked by what other students say in class. Yet when a remark is put into a broader context, such as the context of a religious tradition, it may take on a whole new meaning. Students note that they don't feel they must agree with all religious remarks or observations. Rather, they value the way discussions can be enriched by religious perspectives.

What features do students bring with them when they first arrive on campus? First, if they are religious, regardless of the denomination, they bring a core set of beliefs and traditions. Many bring certain religious rituals that other students may not have encountered before. In classes, such students may interpret literary, historical, or cross-cultural readings in light of their religious upbringing.

And what of students who are not religious? There are many, and, perhaps surprisingly, they show every bit as much enthusiasm for religious diversity as do their more devout friends. Most students who are not religious did not become that way thoughtlessly. They arrived at their views with some reflection. And they are delighted to be informed by fellow students who know more about certain religious traditions. Not proselytized—just informed.

Religious diversity is a bit different from ethnic or other types of diversity among undergraduates. Sara Goldhaber, a student interviewer, concludes from her in-depth interviews with forty religious undergraduates that "given the personal nature of religion, most students learn much more about the religious diversity of their peers through social interactions than they do in class discussions." The students I interviewed echoed this point strongly. And most felt it would be difficult, if not impossible, for the sharing of beliefs and experiences that leads to this personal sort of learning to be built into class discussions. They noted that the nature of classroom discussion at a rigorous college pushes people, understandably, to more academic and abstract conversations and analyses.

Nearly all of the anecdotes students related about learning from religious diversity took place outside of classes. The deeply positive interactions among people of different religions are a striking confirmation of a particular value of a residential college community. Bringing together people from different backgrounds and religions, so that they live together, work together, and play together, leads to an enormous amount of strong positive learning. The evidence is compelling. Goldhaber and I found several kinds of learning from religious diversity.

## REAFFIRMING A RELIGIOUS COMMITMENT

For some students, living in close proximity to others of different religions, or of no religion at all, leads to reflection and insights that reaffirm their own religious faith. One Catholic student told Goldhaber:

I have reevaluated my beliefs. The independence of college life and growing intellectually have been the largest influences for me. These things have made me think more critically about my religious beliefs. They are no longer simply the tradition I was brought up in, and all I know to do. Now, at college, there are people of different religions all around me. And some people have chosen the path of no faith. Living and interacting with these people marks an important difference. Simply seeing myself in contrast to other students, and noticing our differences, has made me reconsider and ultimately reaffirm my faith.

163

Discussions with other students have challenged my beliefs and forced me to explain them. In order to do this well, I have searched for the intellectual bases for my beliefs. I feel I have found them through talking with priests, reading literature, praying, and thinking about issues myself. Part of college is deciding who you are and what you want to be. I think it's the responsibility of every Catholic to seriously consider the priesthood as a vocation. Thinking about this has forced me to think about what is important to me and what drives my life. Friends often come to me to ask about "the Catholic position" on an issue.

For example, in terms of premarital sex, I have learned why the Catholic Church feels it is wrong, rather than just accepting it as dogma. The reasons are both religious and intellectual in basis. Catholics believe that marriage is a sacrament in which man and woman are blessed by God in a special way and only then can engage in sexual intercourse. Also, marriage is a lasting institution, and so sex—as the most intimate expression of physical love—is only appropriate in that context. On other topics, I struggle with the Catholic Church's position, and have questions about the official view. I don't think it is all right to flippantly throw Catholic views out the window, though I do sometimes disagree with the official viewpoint after long consideration of, and struggle over, an issue.

## UNDERSTANDING AND RESPECTING OTHER RELIGIONS

It is natural on a college campus to discuss and examine ideas. And who better to do it with than people who are different from you in some way? When that difference happens to be in religion, students report that they learn a great deal about religions other than their own. Few students have grown up with in-depth knowledge of the customs, traditions, and beliefs of other religions. Living together at college thus provides an ideal environment in which to discuss differing religious perspectives and, even better, to see fellow students practicing their religions. Nearly every student we interviewed expressed respect for fellow students who remain true to their religious traditions even when doing so requires making certain social sacrifices. Seeing friends and colleagues actually implementing customs and beliefs leads to a particularly strong kind of learning.

This theme is brought up repeatedly by students from all religions. It depends heavily on living arrangements, where on a day-to-day basis students from different religious backgrounds and traditions mix and mingle routinely. On a campus where almost any generalization has many exceptions, this learning about different religious traditions seems to be a nearly unanimous feature of residential life.

I grew up in a Christian community, and had never met anyone Jewish before Harvard. When I moved in with a roommate freshman year who observed the major holidays, I learned a lot about the Jewish tradition. It was eye-opening to see the perspective of a different calendar, rules about food, and observance of holiday traditions.

During Passover, I went with my Jewish roommate and another Christian roommate to an interfaith Seder organized by a semi-observant Jew and an Orthodox Jew who were our friends. They invited a Muslim, a Buddhist, a bunch of Christians, and several Jewish friends, so it was a really neat group at the table. We all had the books [Haggadahs], and every time a prayer was read they would go around the table and ask if there was anything similar in our religious traditions.

That was also Holy Week, so I had just come the day before from Good Friday. We had had a similar meal that day to commemorate the Last Supper. I had never really made the connection between the Last Supper and Passover. In Sunday School we had learned that Christ was at a Passover Seder, but if you've never been to one, that means nothing, and is just a trivia fact to pull out. So making connections between these two celebrations, and being with a diverse group of people who were interested in sharing their traditions, was fascinating. It took us hours. We did the entire Passover Seder and in addition all of our interfaith discussions, so we went way longer than the Hillel ones did.

That evening gave me an insight into the figure of Christ that I had never really had. I knew he was Jewish, but realizing that he was at the same type of dinner that I had just experienced for the first time helped me to make sense of why all of his apostles were together and drinking wine and eating bread—actually, matzo. In the prayer book there's a line the priest says every week during Eucharist that quotes Christ saying, "Take, eat, and every time you do this, do this in remembrance of me," or something to that effect. I had never understood that choice of wording. First of all, I thought "this" meant eating in general, and then I realized that it came from the Passover meal, which of course happens only once a year and so had a more special origin.

In addition, I had thought his words were a bit egotistical and should have been ringing alarm bells in the disciples' heads about Christ's coming death. But I realized in the context of the Passover Seder that saying something so important would not be unusual because the rest of the Seder is also of tremendous import. Seeing this special and spiritual meal put Christ's words in a context that made more sense and had new meaning to me. I feel that now I have a whole basis for understanding another religion.

## EXPLORING ONE'S OWN BELIEFS

The college years are a time of change, introspection, questioning, and exploration of what a student believes in—and religious diversity can help this exploration. One woman spoke to Goldhaber from the midst of this process:

Everything that I have learned by observing and interacting with my more religious roommates has helped me to decide what is important and not important to me in a belief system, or more generally in a spiritual outlook. I have a specific example.

My observant Protestant roommate got married to a very religious person who wants to be a minister and to participate in religion within a framework that I feel is blatantly sexist. When my roommate was deciding to marry him, I felt very uncomfortable with the idea. Her wedding made me realize that what is important to me in my religious quest is not to find fault with the religions of other people, but rather to interact with people in a loving, caring way. I learned to look past, and to forgive, the aspects of other people's religions and beliefs that I may disagree with.

This process forced me to think hard about what I believe. If I really believe that people carry God within them and are sentient beings, oppression didn't matter. To think that a sexist attitude would oppress people would be to deny the spiritual power of individuals. Yet I am still uncomfortable with this view that I came to, because it commits me to a view of the world that is counterintuitive for me. I am a liberal, and I work to decrease poverty and suffering and oppression in many situations. So it is hard to justify my work while believing in the spiritual framework I just described. I think this all requires a transformation of my perception of suffering, one which I am far from mastering.

## BONDS BETWEEN RELIGIOUS STUDENTS

Students of strong religious faith often forge a unique bond and develop a special respect for the commitment of deeply religious students from other faiths and from other ethnic groups. One student expressed this especially well:

> As a Catholic, I find there is a certain bond that exists for me with observant people of other religions. Interfaith forums have certainly helped to develop this connection with the other side, such as Jewish students from Hillel with whom we share many events. In making tough moral decisions, it's often helpful to look at people who are devout in another religion, for example Judaism, and to see that they have a lot of parallel structures. We also share some of the funny parts of religious culture, like Catholic or Jewish guilt.
>
> I definitely feel comfortable talking about certain things, or taking certain things for granted, when I'm with other religious people, whatever their religion. That's the key point. For example, another religious person would have more understanding of a politically less popular view on abortion, or birth control, even if they didn't personally agree with my view. They would un-

derstand it is part of a commitment I have made that shapes my life. Also, a major part of my life is going to church and participating in the Catholic Students Association, which Protestant students at Christian Fellowship and Jewish students at Hillel can relate to their own experiences.

## LINKING CLASS DISCUSSIONS TO PERSONAL LIFE

When religious ideas come up in class discussions, students often perceive links between the discussions and their own beliefs and personal lives. The result is a blending that is delicate and occasionally even risks offense. Yet that tension can help students connect the academic and personal facets of their lives. A young man told Goldhaber:

> In a course called "Justice," I often felt that my own views on moral reasoning were not *tabula rasa*, but rather they were highly influenced by my religious beliefs. In sections and in papers, when we were asked to describe which philosopher we agreed with and why, I found myself searching for the theory that was closest to my religious views. It felt awkward to have to hide my religious views, and to try to disguise them in secular philosophy. The professor was not at all at fault. It just seemed that this course did not call for religious foundations of philosophy.
>
> For example, I understood my own reasoning for treating people well through the saying "Love thy neighbor as thou love thyself," a religious platitude from the New Testament said by Jesus. However, in communicating my views to my peers, I had to find a secular philosophical argument, going back to a social contract theory of obligations to other citizens. This

didn't capture the essence of my feelings exactly, because this translates to "I won't hit my neighbors because I don't want to be hit," which isn't the same as loving your neighbors, regardless of whether or not they want to love you.

I believe this student raises a challenge for both students and faculty on most college campuses. Religious students face a genuine difficulty when they think about connecting their personal religious beliefs with academic work in classrooms. There is something special about religion that makes it different from most other perspectives or opinions or beliefs. Sara Goldhaber, while summarizing her overwhelmingly positive findings about the impact of religious differences on students' learning, both academic and personal, states the challenge very directly:

> It becomes a continuing challenge to make the campus atmosphere as welcoming as possible to productive religious discourse and sharing. For example, most students, staff, and administrators would say that a diverse student body is valuable because part of a modern college education is learning about the different backgrounds and ideas of other students. If a Vietnamese student invited a group of friends or a class to a demonstration of Vietnamese cooking and culture, most people would find the invitation to be a great offer, even if they didn't have time to attend. However, if a Catholic invited the same people to a church service or discussion group, many people might be turned off, or might even interpret the invitation to be proselytizing, and thus feel threatened by it.

The fundamental difference between religion and other types of diversity is that it involves deeply held beliefs, rather than important experiences (as in a culture) or physical characteristics (as in a race). Therefore, even if religious students try to share their experiences, without any strings attached, in an attempt to educate others about different ways of living in this world, they may not always be received kindly.

Another difference between religious and cultural or racial diversity follows from the core belief systems of religions. While most people are eager to experience or observe cultural practices different from their own, many are reluctant to do the same with religion. This reluctance seems to stem from two feelings. First, one's religious beliefs may forbid participating in another religion. Or if one is an atheist, this may prevent one from seeing value in any religion. Second, people outside of a religion may be reluctant to challenge or even to discuss any of its beliefs or practices, because of a sense that the discussion will be futile or their basic knowledge insufficient.

Goldhaber is not exaggerating the challenges faced by religious students and the value of efforts by college leaders to make students from various religions feel welcome and comfortable on campus. A short comment from a devout Jewish student hints at some of those challenges and reveals one young woman's way of coping with them:

I consciously didn't take a single course on Judaism in my entire time at Harvard. Primarily, I was not interested in exploring my own tradition, in an academic, institutional context, especially at a Christian-founded university like Harvard. This is certainly still a Protestant institution at its core. For example, when you walk into Sanders Theatre, the emblems on the wall still say "Christos et Ecclesia." And the fact that there's a big church in the middle of Harvard Yard represents a part of this institution. I don't mind these things, but they are not accidental, and do reflect the values of the university.

Secondarily, I made this choice because I had come to college to learn something new. What I came here for was an intellectual exploration, and I have seen this exploration as being opposed to an emotional and personal exploration. Therefore, by definition, I feel that an academic journey must involve analytical distance. I was unwilling to explore Judaism, my own religion, because I felt that it would require an analytical distance from my own tradition that I don't have and don't want to have.

I still think that people should feel comfortable sharing their personal religious views. My decision not to study Judaism at Harvard was not because I didn't think Harvard could accommodate my discussion of Judaism, but rather because I didn't think my feeling about Judaism could accommodate Harvard.

Overall, as noted earlier, students report that the impact of religious diversity on campus is deeply positive. Goldhaber summarizes what she learned from interviews with her fellow students:

I certainly heard some truthful reports of tensions caused by religious diversity, as well as reports of a lack of contact with people of other religions. However, the overwhelming sense was one of positive interaction and growing mutual respect. Respect grows and negative stereotypes are dispelled. This positive result is exactly what I was told by every one of the ten Catholics, ten Protestants, ten Jews, and ten Muslims whom I interviewed. I was stunned by their strong unanimity. They all had gotten to know someone at Harvard who, on a personal level, increased their knowledge of, and often respect for, a certain religious group. Interviewees valued their contact with people of other religions for various reasons. Many emphasized the power of meeting real people to dispel negative impressions imprinted by common stereotypes, media simplifications, or political agendas.

## Living and Learning Together

When preparing to ask about learning related to students' different ethnic and racial backgrounds, I expected to find that most "academic" learning took place in classes and most "personal" learning happened in interactions outside of classes. Student interviewers predicted that the interviews would confound my expectations. They were right. Learning does not take place in such a partitioned way.

Perhaps because of this crossover between in-class and out-of-class learning, when students interact with fellow students from different racial and ethnic backgrounds in day-to-day living, it makes a strong impression. This finding drives home the importance of creating residential living arrangements that bring students from different backgrounds together, rather than creating separation by racial or ethnic background. If students from different backgrounds live apart from one another, a precious kind of learning may be lost.

Students give myriad examples of such crossovers between in-class learning and residential living, and they characterize them as highlights of their life at college. One striking story comes from a junior:

I'm an African-American guy who grew up in a pretty middle-class home. I went to an integrated high school. I thought I knew exactly what to expect here at college when I got my freshman roommate mailing. There were going to be four of us—two white and two black, in a suite with three small bedrooms. So two guys get singles, and two share a bedroom. I wondered how that would work, and expected it might cause some tension. I especially hoped the tension wouldn't be anything racial.

As it turns out, I was completely wrong about what would happen. We quickly resolved the room arrangements by agreeing to split the year with two of us sharing for the first half and the other two sharing for the second half. So that potential dilemma vanished quickly. For the first few weeks the four of all got along quite well.

But it was the connection with our classes that created some tensions. One of my white roommates and I both enrolled in a literature class where we read work by a diverse group of writers. And this was where the academic work and our living together intersected. It made for some difficult moments.

I remember two examples in particular. We read two black authors, and, to say the least, their styles were very different. One was a piece by Imamu Amiri Baraka called "The Toilet." The other was an essay by James Baldwin, written when he lived in Paris. I thought Baraka was a challenging and complex writer, while I was disappointed with Baldwin. My white roommate had exactly the opposite reaction.

Now you could say that this is entirely normal. Why would anyone be surprised that two students would have different takes on two authors? But somehow when we talked about it, we both got very offended. I had assumed he would agree with me, and he had assumed I would agree with him. Then he called the Baraka piece "absolute trash," and I took it as a racial remark. So I clammed up and stopped talking to him. Our relationship became very strained.

Thank goodness for our two other roommates. It was pretty obvious to both of them what was happening. One evening a few days later they just couldn't stand the tension. So when we had our regular weekly "group grousing time" they pressed each of us.

I first realized that evening that if I become angry with a white guy who really is a good guy, it's pretty foolish for me to think he is a racist just because he doesn't like a particular piece of writing by a black man. How would I feel if I told my white roommate I didn't enjoy reading James Joyce, and he accused me of making a racist remark? I would get upset with him, and I think I would be right to get upset with him.

The good news is that the four of us are still living together now, as juniors. And thanks to those awkward moments we had together as freshmen, now I feel completely free to criticize James Michener or James Joyce or Henry James, and my white roommate feels completely free to say what he really thinks about any black author. We even laugh about it now, because it's kind of a bond. It's hard for me to advise other people to live together the way our group has done. But I can certainly say that for me, as one guy, the intersection of living arrangement and academic work has been a big learning experience, a big winner.

Another student in his junior year gave the following example to interviewer Anna Fincke:

Freshman year I had one roommate who was black. We became very close friends. We find each other easier to associate with than many other people.

Being white, I think having a black roommate freshman year has had an impact on the mix of people I know. I met people he knew. I don't think that's unusual—any roommate who runs in a different crowd will bring that.

He was from Georgia and had a very strong tradition of African-American culture. He was quite religious and conservative. He really represents to me some especially interesting, valuable, and worthy aspects of African-American traditions. In discussions I became aware of some of his struggles and the circumstances he encounters. Like in my high school there was a considerable rift between blacks and whites in terms of academics. It's interesting to see how he dealt with those difficulties.

I don't think anyone comes here without preconceived notions. They arise from your life experience. And they always change with your new experiences. The high school I went to was racially mixed—it was just over half black. The chance to get to know students of other races here, and have challenging, searching discussions with them, has raised my confidence in asserting who I am and what I believe, without respect to race. In a small town in Texas, where I'm from, it's easy to fall into certain unfortunate patterns of talking to people of different races. There are certain formalisms used to smooth over tensions. Now I'm more willing to be direct and inclined to say what I think is the truth about one issue or another.

For each student, the tone of college life is set early. Much of that tone depends upon roommates, neighbors, and dorm supervisors. Again, living arrangements go a long way toward shaping both attitudes and relationships. A young woman told Sara Goldhaber about an unexpected friendship:

Moving into our dorms freshman year, we all got together the first night in our proctor's room. She had asked us to bring something along that was important to us, and to introduce it along with ourselves. I had just come back from spending a summer traveling through Eastern Europe and Israel. My object was a pillow. When I was young, my best friend was an Israeli girl whose family had moved to America for a few years. That summer I had visited them in Israel. When I left, the younger kids presented me with a red, heart-shaped pillow they had made. It said in Hebrew, "Have a safe trip. We love you," and it had all their names on it. It really meant something to me. I thought the pillow was very emblematic of both my relationships with people and my religious experiences.

Just before my turn, the guy next to me introduced himself as a Shiite Muslim from Pakistan. His object was a necklace with several pendants of Koranic verses and a curved sword. I was stunned. I hadn't ever had direct contact with a Muslim before, and I had such a historical prejudice and fear of negative interactions between Jews and Muslims.

Shocked and frightened a bit, I went on anyway with what I was going to say, and explained that I was a religious Jew. He turned to me with a big grin and said, "Great! It's always hard to find somebody else who doesn't want pepperoni on their pizza." We became fast friends and it was always a big joke that we could go out to dinner together, because we had similar dietary restrictions.

Meeting the Muslim guy in my dorm turned Islam into a real religion for me. After being a fanatical ideal, it became something which real people practiced and believed in. This experience made me realize the prejudices that I held about religion in general, and Islam in particular. Before meeting him, I was frankly unwilling to believe that he could keep his Muslim views out of any discussion. I see people make this misguided assumption all the time, because when someone says they are religious, it is easy to jump to the conclusion that that is the only thing which defines them.

Living with students from different backgrounds can actually change behavior. In the spirit of pressing students to go beyond platitudes when talking about the impact of residential living, I asked interviewees to give examples of interactions from their residential living experience that changed their behavior. Two seniors who lived in the same residence hall both told me of a particular incident. It illustrates the power of roommates, the value of choosing wisely, and how residential living experiences can change behavior. One of the seniors described the incident this way:

Eight of us blocked together. Eight guys. Four of us are white, one is black, three are Asian. We were all just chatting on a weekend afternoon. We had known each other since freshman year. Saw each other practically every day. Didn't expect any big surprises. We feel entirely comfortable with each other.

It was last October. I remember one of the Asian guys

asked, "How are you going to handle voting in the November election? Are you going home, or are you going to use an absentee ballot?" All five of us non-Asian guys responded that we hadn't thought about it yet. The truth is that a couple of us might just have let the election slide. We are pretty busy. And since none of us come from cities or towns right near campus, I guess we would have just let this one election pass.

The Asian-American guys became visibly upset. They asked how much we knew about Au Sung Aung Ky. Two of us knew she was the Burmese woman under house arrest who had won a Nobel Peace Prize while fighting for democracy in Burma. They asked us if we had heard about Wang Dan, who was arrested in China's Tienanmen Square student uprising for democracy. They asked about Wei-Jing Shei, sitting in jail because of his speaking out and writing for democracy in China. They pressed us how, knowing about these people and what they were risking for the chance to vote, while we were taking so much for granted—how could we just take a pass on voting that year?

Well, it didn't take them long to embarrass us. Big time. They didn't try to rub our noses in it, or anything like that. But they felt strongly about it. They certainly changed our behavior. So the five of us all made a big point of sending away for absentee ballots that very afternoon. And all five of us voted. Now that I think back on that afternoon, it seemed like a small thing at the time. But it really affected me. I bet you I will never pass on another election in my lifetime.

For learning—and behavior change—to take place, students must mix and mingle and interact. Ideally students from different backgrounds should work together to accomplish a common task. Sometimes formally in a classroom. Often less formally outside of classes. The key point is that extensive contact, preferably both inside and outside of class, is what allows students to benefit and learn from ethnic differences on campus—and that residential arrangements can foster this contact in a way that encourages such learning.

## A Measure of Interethnic Interaction

If in order to learn from one another, students of different backgrounds must spend time together, it may be useful to discover how much time students actually spend with people from backgrounds unlike their own. Students and campus leaders at any college may wish to investigate this question.

At many colleges, there is no doubt that students from different ethnic groups mix and mingle routinely in classes. Yet naturally the extent of such mingling varies. To explore the extent of such interaction at Harvard, we agreed, after much thought, on a simple first-cut indicator. We decided to ask about roommate choices: What fraction of students choose to live with other students from different racial and ethnic backgrounds?

At Harvard, all first-year students are assigned to live with one or more roommates or suitemates. These assignments are made with great thought and care by the Freshman Dean's Office, and most rooming groups include some ethnic diversity. I know many other residential colleges use similar procedures. But after that first year, students decide for themselves whom to live with.

We therefore asked a random sample of graduating seniors

one question: Had they ever chosen to live with a roommate of a different ethnic group from their own? Each student was to answer the question with a simple yes or no. We made clear that in using the phrase "different ethnic group" we were thinking of four main groups: whites, blacks, Asians, and Latinos. We did not define, say, a Jewish white student choosing to live with a Methodist white student as choosing someone from a different ethnic group.

We discovered that 78 percent of the seniors had chosen to live with at least one person from a different ethnic group at some point during their college years. When I shared this finding with Dr. Dean Whitla, who then ran Harvard's Office of Instructional Research and Development, he told me he had done a similar study and had found the answer to be 76 percent. So whatever the precise result to the second decimal place, we can say with confidence the fraction of our students who choose multiethnic living groups is high.

This pattern of choosing to live with people from different racial and ethnic groups is a positive step toward maximizing informal interactions. One clear illustration of the power and importance of living arrangements on campus emerged when I asked a religious Jewish student the question about roommate choice. He lived in a group of four. His three roommates were a Christian, a Muslim, and a Hindu. All four were religiously observant. Two had light skin, and two had dark skin. All had visited one another's homes outside of college.

This young man took obvious pleasure in describing how much each of the four had learned about the other three religions from this living arrangement. He said he had taken two formal courses on world religions, which had been entirely satisfactory and well taught. Yet, he stressed, he had learned far more from the day-to-day interactions and conversations with his suitemates than he ever could have learned from any abstract readings.

## Difficult Trade-offs

For some undergraduates, the hardest kind of learning comes from choices they must make that arise from living in close proximity to people from backgrounds different from their own. There is disagreement even among the most thoughtful students about what friendship patterns and what dating patterns are right for them.

While students may learn much from talking, living, and studying with fellow undergraduates from different racial and ethnic groups, each must make certain trade-offs between competing expectations from friends and family. The racially diverse backgrounds of students on campus lead to pressures on each student, some remarkably direct and some more subtle. These pressures force students to think carefully about how they will deal with certain conflicts.

Several African-American interviewees talked about pressures they had faced concerning how they would organize their social lives on campus. Each of these students specifically mentioned the conflict between "integrationist" and "separatist" pressures from friends on campus, and occasionally even from friends back home. They referred to an essay they had read by Henry Louis Gates Jr. in which Professor Gates recalls, twenty-five years later, what it was like for him to arrive at Yale College as a black first-year student. These undergraduates identified this essay as capturing some of the challenge of their own experience. They urged fellow students to read it, because, they say, once friendship patterns are established in the early months at college it is difficult to make major changes.

Several students identified pressures from other sources that forced them to make difficult personal decisions. A striking example comes from a Korean-American student from California. When asked about how diversity on campus had affected her, either academically or personally, she focused immediately on the personal impact:

I bet you are hearing lots of uplifting sagas about how exposure to people from different backgrounds forces us to rethink assumptions and enhances the quality of all of our lives. Well, I am an example of someone who certainly is being forced to rethink assumptions, but I am less sure about how it is affecting the quality of my life. In fact, dealing with diversity is probably the hardest part of coming to terms with what I value most.

I will tell you about the conversation I had with my mother as we flew here before freshman week, on the airplane from California. My mother is a traditional, Korean woman. She works very hard and retains strong family values. She certainly has inculcated these values in me, as a central part of my life. Well, on the plane she got to talking about her hopes for my romantic life. And she was remarkably specific. She said she hoped I would only date certain people. And then she rank ordered them.

She hoped most that I would meet a Korean-American guy. Then a Chinese American. Then any other Asian American. After that, maybe, just maybe, a white guy. No one else made it over the threshold. I don't think she considered what she was telling me as controversial in any way. It was the way she had been brought up, herself. She said that family is everything, and that this mattered more than anything else, to her and to my father.

183

Can you imagine what impact this had on my arrival here? I felt that I couldn't let any man who is not an Asian American even get to know me too well. What would I do if he asked me to a party, or wanted to build a closer relationship? Of course I understood that following my parents' wishes would have a social cost, and would constrain my circle of friends.

But I feel like my parents practically sacrificed their own lives for me so that I could get a great education and come here. I found this very difficult to grapple with. Here, everyone talks about diversity and all its benefits, while my parents made just one request— choose to date only men who are like you.

I have thought about this dilemma constantly in my years here, and finally made a decision that I believe is the right one for me. Maybe not for others, but for me. I decided that honoring my parents and their request is the one way I can repay them for what they have done for me. So even though this decision limits my social life, and some of my friends disagree, I am following their wish.

I don't know whether you would judge that I made a good or a bad decision. What I do know, since you began by asking about the impact of ethnic diversity here at college on me, is that I have never been forced to think harder about something than about this dilemma. And it is the diversity here that forced me to dig deep into my soul and try to figure out what is right for me. I know that I will be rethinking this conclusion from time to time. But for now, I feel content in my soul that honoring my parents' wish is more important than any other choice I could make.

## Learning about Oneself

In the context of residential living, some students inevitably encounter situations in which they are uncomfortable. This characterizes life at any college. And it was true long before colleges began to strive for diversity in their student bodies. Yet when students from different racial or ethnic backgrounds live together, new kinds of delicate moments and personal interactions inevitably arise. While some of these circumstances can be difficult for students to cope with, students from all backgrounds report that they learn something. Often that something is about themselves.

Several graduating seniors commented on the importance of the simple principle of bringing good will to all personal encounters. For example, a young white woman suggested that one way to enhance good will among people of different backgrounds is to encourage each student to be *reflective* about himself. Especially when racial or ethnic differences raise a delicate issue or lead to an awkward moment. Inevitably these awkward moments will occur. It is up to each student to transform them into an educational opportunity—a learning experience.

When a student is willing to be reflective and assume good will, the results can be powerful. To illustrate this, the young woman told a personal story:

> You ask for my experience with diversity, both the good and the not so good. I want to start with a not so good. I think I learned more from that not-so-good experience, especially about myself, than from some of the nicest ones.
>
> Here is what happened. It was during sophomore year. One day at lunch, I saw a woman whom I considered a

185

friend, sitting and having lunch with three other students. This girl happened to be an African American, and so were her lunch companions. I didn't know anyone else nearby, so I asked if I could join them, and my friend said sure. The four of them then continued to talk to one another, and basically ignored me. This continued for at least fifteen minutes, until I felt so uncomfortable that I said "See you later" and got up and just left with my tray and my not quite finished meal.

It really bothered me. I thought first, that they were rude; second, that the woman I considered my friend wasn't really my friend; and third, that it must be something racial. I stewed about it for days. Then I screwed up my courage and asked this maybe friend to sit with me for a few minutes. I told her my version of what happened, and asked her straight out if it was something racial or something else, and said that I thought she was my friend, but didn't understand her behavior and was genuinely hurt. It was not what I would call an uplifting moment.

Well, the conversation we had gave me a whole new insight into myself. And into how people can hurt one another without meaning to. My friend was clearly surprised by what I told her. She had assumed that it was obvious to me what was happening at the lunch table. This group of four students had a regular Tuesday lunch session, where they discussed their student association activities and plans.

She explained to me that when I sat down and joined them, they didn't mind a bit, but they were trying to get some planning done, and they were in the middle of it. So they didn't want to be rude to me and say, "Go away, we're busy," but they didn't want to break the continuity of their planning, either. They had been working on a project together, each Tuesday lunch, for many weeks.

My friend then asked me a question that set me back. Suppose, she asked, I had instead joined four white women, over that same lunch, who were in the middle of discussing their homework for their literature class, or chemistry class, or planning for their a capella group concert, or any other such thing. And these four women met over lunch every Tuesday for this purpose. Would you expect to be immediately included? And, if my answer was no, if it would have been obvious to me that I was joining an ongoing discussion, why wasn't it equally obvious with the four African-American women?

Could it be, my black friend said kind of gently, that you put a racial overlay onto a thoroughly nonracial situation, and that it is *your* assumption about some racial component to this event, even though it wasn't there, that shaped your interpretation?

I had never thought of it that way. And the more I thought about it, the more complicated it became. This interaction forced me to ask myself some tough questions about my own assumptions. I also learned two lessons for the future. One lesson is that in the future, if I were one of those four women, whatever their race, I would explain to the newcomer, meaning me, that the four of us were pursuing an ongoing planned conversation. Had one of them simply told me that before I sat down, the whole incident would have been avoided.

The second lesson is for me to think twice before laying a racial or ethnic overlay onto a situation that could have happened in exactly the same way with four white women. I think that is the thing that people need to think about. It is way too easy to fall into those traps.

The theme of learning about themselves is one many undergraduates bring up when I ask about how diversity at college has affected them. Interactions among students of different races and ethnicities leads to some unexpected, sometimes difficult, occasionally jarring insights about oneself. This is a serious, deep, powerful kind of learning. It is often more personal than academic. Here is what one African-American senior had to say, two weeks before graduation, about the diversity he encountered on campus:

> They are going to have to carry me kicking and screaming out of this place. I have had experiences here that I worry I will never be able to have in such a full way again. You ask about the impact on me, as an African-American guy, of living in a diverse community like Harvard's. I am happy to share my thoughts about this.
>
> When I first arrived here, I was sure the biggest impact on me, in connection with the word "diversity," which I heard until it was coming out of my ears, would come from meeting lots of white and Asian and Latino students who would be different from me. That has happened. On the whole it has been good. Whatever minor imperfections I could describe, I will be forever grateful to this place for giving me an incredible opportunity.
>
> But while that was what I expected, and it was what happened, it was not the biggest deal, at least for me personally. I went to school in Washington, D.C. I went to an independent school that had a handful of black students. There were four of us in my graduating class. I did not grow up in a rich neighborhood. Kind of the opposite. And most of my neighborhood friends were very different from me.

It was hard. I really cared about school. I loved that place too, and worked my tail off. Most of the guys I grew up with, in the neighborhood, just didn't. They did the opposite. I was constantly swimming upstream. I was the oddball. Even in school, and it was a really good school, with so few blacks, again I sometimes felt like the odd man out.

Here at college, the impact of student diversity has been incredibly powerful for me, in a way I never expected. From the first week I got here, I realized I was one of many dozens of African-American students who are smart, academically motivated, in fact I would even say driven. Until I got here, it wasn't obvious to me that there even are dozens, indeed hundreds, of people who not only look like me, but who share so many of my values. Especially in terms of sustained academic work. I had simply never seen it while growing up. This was the first place I ever saw it.

I don't know if that answers your question about the impact of diversity. But for me this has probably been the single most powerful effect. Just being exposed to dozens of fellow African Americans who share so many of my values is something I will always be grateful to Harvard for. The result is a very personal feeling, and it helps me to define who I am. And that never occurred to me before I got here as something connected in any way to the word "diversity."

# 9

## WHAT COLLEGE LEADERS CAN DO

As part of each interview, we invited undergraduates to make suggestions to deans and other campus leaders about policies that would improve student life on campus. Students have no shortage of suggestions. We always pressed for specific examples from their own experience to illustrate why they thought a particular suggestion would work. Several students, when mentioning these ideas, volunteered that their suggestions might not have occurred to them when they first arrived at college. Apparently, making suggestions to deans is an acquired taste.

### A Policy of Inclusion

To learn from one another, students from different backgrounds, and from different racial or ethnic groups, must interact. If campus norms encourage students to develop groups built primarily on race or ethnicity, interactions across groups become harder. Students describe a particular aspect of Harvard College that differs more from their high schools than nearly any other aspect they can think of. It is the college leadership's insistence that activities on campus be inclusive.

Students dwell on this point for two reasons. First, for many, this is an idea on which their own thinking has evolved during their time at college. Many students, especially nonwhite students, report that when they arrived they were dismayed at not finding a Third World Center or a Women's Center or a Multicultural Center. Some students, even as seniors, remain dismayed. A significant group of non-white seniors say they see value in having such a gathering place.

Yet a solid majority of the nonwhite students, and nearly all the white students, report an evolution in their feelings about making it too easy for individuals to withdraw into the friendly confines of a physical space where everyone else looks like them. Many seniors comment that if they had withdrawn to a Third World Center they would have missed many learning opportunities. Several feel more strongly. One African-American senior explained emphatically:

> The student diversity here is a big reason I came to Harvard. If I wanted to spend most or all of my time with people who look just like me, it would have been quite straightforward to arrange. I would have gone to Howard instead of Harvard.

A second reason some students recommend a policy of inclusion is that they believe such a policy sends a message. It sets a tone. It affects the way first-year students allocate their time. And a campus-wide policy of inclusion stimulates other, unplanned actions by students. One junior, who was studying economics, termed such unplanned actions "externalities" of a policy that stresses inclusion.

An illustration of such an externality was given to interviewer Sara Goldhaber by a junior who was Jewish by birth yet had grown up as a Unitarian. His three first-year roommates were a Catholic, a Protestant, and an observant Buddhist from Korea. He told Goldhaber about his celebration of the Jewish holiday of Passover:

Two years ago I ran an interethnic Seder, to which I invited my roommates and other friends. Passover had been one of the few religious holidays I actually participated in while growing up. I had a Hagaddah [booklet for the ceremony] that my cousin had compiled. I made a "kosher for Passover" pizza for the dinner, and put together a Seder plate, which contains several symbolic items. I answered questions about the meaning of different items. When people asked about yarmulkes, I gave them the choice of whether to wear one or not.

This goes back to the issue of what significance a foreign ritual can have for someone, and even whether their practice of this ritual dilutes its meaning for those who truly practice it. On the other hand, participating in rituals develops knowledge and understanding, which is very important. So I am conscious of both sharing and privacy issues.

But there was no real hierarchy or leader. We simply all sat around the table and took turns reading passages. People were very excited about the Seder the entire way through, and especially enjoyed the spirited singing.

This student makes a point about inclusion, and how it sets a tone for everyone and an attitude toward life on campus. The tone is that it is quite natural for students from different backgrounds to learn from one another. This young man is clearly arguing that such a tone enhances respect for differences, rather than sparking some sort of anger about them. He concluded by telling Goldhaber:

I worked at the student-run university Lutheran homeless shelter. We use the basement of the Lutheran church, but the shelter itself is secular. As a supervisor, I would run the shelter overnight quite often. There were a lot of sensitivity issues there, including that of religion. I had a very dedicated team of volunteers, but we were still short on help, and it was difficult to fill some days. When holidays came up, it was hard to find replacements. It was a source of tension only in that it was inconvenient to find replacements, but everyone was sensitive to other people's religious needs.

When students share examples like these they often include the caveat that they realize it takes a certain courage, both from deans and from student leaders, especially leaders of ethnic group organizations, to insist on a policy of inclusion. Several undergraduates report having discussions with friends on other campuses and learning that policies differ sharply from one college to another. They point out that differences in campus policies have real consequences, and that both academic and personal learning on any campus is influenced by the extent to which inclusion is implemented both formally by campus leaders and less formally by students.

The consequences of a policy of inclusion transcend platitudes and translate into concrete evidence that often surprises observers. I learned from students at Hillel that a significant number of active participants in the Hillel Drama Society are not Jewish. I learned from one of the African-American leaders of the Kuumba Singers that all undergraduates are welcome. So while the spirit of African-American joy and celebration radiates from their performances, all students on campus come to feel this is a "campus event," and not solely a "black students' event." This is what one of the Kuumba Singers' leaders had to say:

Isn't it ironic how we increase the power and effect of our work by simply opening it up to everyone. Obviously the majority of singers are going to be black. That's not a surprise. What surprised me most is how many whites wanted to join us. We didn't take everyone who tried out, but we did take a bunch. The main criterion was simply that we wanted people with good spirit and people who could sing. And our audiences were among the biggest on campus. I think maybe we get such big audiences because we include some whites and Asians in the group. I get a real bang out of watching some of the black parents' mouths drop open, including my own parents, when they see us all first come out on stage, at the beginning of our performance, and about a third of the group are white! Certainly at least a third of our audiences are white too. And that really makes me feel good. Unexpectedly good. I don't know if we are teaching or just entertaining, but either way it is one of the best parts of being here.

No one suggests that a policy of inclusion be carried to foolish extremes. While ethnic group organizations may sponsor many open and inclusive events, for example, no student suggests that the president of the Asian-American Students Association be Latino, or the other way around. I suspect all readers understand very well the main point of the students' suggestion for a policy of inclusion. The hard question is whether campus leaders, both students and administrators, have the courage to implement such a policy.

## Building a Campus Culture

Campuses really do have unique cultures. I once asked a distinguished anthropologist if he could explain why faculty members at some colleges seem to care deeply about the effectiveness of their teaching, while colleagues at other similar colleges clearly care less. He responded, "It's in the air." When I pressed him harder, he said, "I think it's a combination of history, faculty values, leadership, and student expectations."

Students offer a similar answer when asked under what circumstances students from different backgrounds learn most, in the most natural way, from one another. Many students feel that diversity appears to be working reasonably well on our campus. To what do they attribute this good outcome? A significant number give the credit to campus culture builders (my choice of phrase, not theirs). They describe a relentless effort by these culture builders to encourage all students to take full advantage of campus diversity. This does not happen with segregated clubs. It does not happen with segregated arts activities or singing groups or drama productions. It happens when students as well as campus leaders make a proactive effort to capitalize on the opportunities diversity offers.

When students refer in their interviews to those who build campus culture, they do not just mean deans or residence hall directors or leaders of student organizations. They describe a variety of situations in which a person with no official title made a difference. They are really characterizing *every student*, in the old-fashioned sense of believing that each person can make a difference by setting an example.

Interviewer Robert Eng found an example of this in his talk with an Asian-American woman, a sophomore concentrating in biochemistry. She told him about having played a leadership role in her high school. Her story makes the point that one student leader can, by making an effort, make a difference.

As Eng tells us, this young woman was from rural Georgia, a racially segregated town where hers was the only family that was neither black nor white. He quotes her words:

> There were a lot of undertones of white supremacy where I lived. I felt a lot of racial prejudice but I also felt that they really didn't know how to deal with me because I was kind of new and foreign. But I got along very well with everyone and I didn't have problems socially relating to them. Yet I think there was still a lot of tension.

In this atmosphere, the public high school had two homecoming queens, one black and one white. Then the young woman took action:

> I was class president, and so my senior year I managed to convince the Board of Education that having a Black Homecoming Queen and a White Homecoming Queen was not very good for student relations. Through a lot of work, I was able to eliminate that. So now there is only one Queen. And isn't that funny? I wasn't even eligible. I mean, just because people are not kind to you doesn't give you a reason to be unkind to them.

Students have a specific suggestion for campus culture builders, and it is clear that this suggestion would work on many college campuses. It is that deans and other adults should convey to all incoming students that they have a once-in-a-lifetime opportunity to experience, in their college years, a new set of people with new ideas that may challenge their own. They should encourage students to see these few precious years as a special chance to meet, work with, and get to know others who are unlike themselves. A number of students brought up a particular event that had conveyed this message to them.

During the summer before their first year at Harvard, incoming freshmen receive a booklet in the mail. The booklet contains several essays. In one recent year these essays included one by our college president about how civility can transform the process of living together into a great learning experience; one by Henry Louis Gates Jr. about what it was like to enter college and feel conflicting pressures from different groups on campus; one by Henry David Thoreau on self-reliance and maintaining one's own integrity; one by Anne Fadiman on keeping an open mind about different perspectives, especially when interpreting great literature; and several by undergraduates from various ethnic groups about their experiences at college in seeking common ground. The shared theme of these essays is that finding common ground is often a challenge and requires continuing effort. It does not just happen.

Students are asked to read these essays, and before first-semester classes begin, faculty members who have volunteered for this role meet with groups of about twenty students from different backgrounds to discuss the readings. The purpose is to invite students to think together about how they will deal with the diversity of students they see around them every day. This program is now several years old, and more than two hundred faculty members have volunteered to spend a morning during the first week with the new students.

This program is a particularly simple example. Any campus could implement it. And many students mention it as an instance of how campus culture builders can set a tone and get students thinking about a search for common ground. Replicated in different ways by different campus leaders, a tone is set both for students and for all other members of a campus community. Students find this a particularly constructive and important step toward helping themselves, and their fellows, feel that a sense of pleasure in reaching out to people different from themselves is natural—it is just "in the air."

## Leaders of Student Groups

It is not surprising that most undergraduates, when invited to make suggestions about how any campus can most constructively and effectively facilitate learning among a diverse group of students, immediately focus on what others should do. They offer suggestions for faculty members. They offer suggestions for deans. They offer suggestions for residence hall leaders and professors and other staff members. Most of these suggestions are superb, and I report them throughout this book.

But what can students themselves do to facilitate learning from others of different backgrounds? What suggestions do students have for their fellow students, especially student leaders? Two sets of ideas come up repeatedly. The first is the important role ethnic group and racial group organizations, and their leaders, can play in making campus diversity an actively positive force. The second concerns the attitude with which each student approaches life on campus.

### ETHNIC AND RACIAL ORGANIZATIONS

Students list several ways in which ethnic, racial, and religious organizations can contribute to campus life. Of the 120 seniors I interviewed, 91 felt these organizations already play highly constructive roles on our campus. Everyone understands that the primary purpose of each student organization, the reason it exists in the first place, is to offer students from a certain background or religion or race or ethnicity a place to meet, mingle with, and enjoy friends from similar backgrounds. The way such organizations operate, when at their best, gets particularly high marks from just about every student who is involved with one or more of them. Even more striking, students who are *not* actively involved give them high marks for making *all* members of the campus community feel welcome. This is a wonderful finding to report.

One set of student suggestions to make these organizations even more effective centers around sponsorship of events. Some may be academic events, such as inviting a speaker to come to campus. Others may be more elaborate, such as an ongoing series of speakers. Still others may be social events. Many students say it is critical for leaders of student organizations to keep in mind that they have an opportunity to make major contributions to the campus as a whole, going beyond just their organizations' members, when they create or sponsor or organize cultural events. Such events give any group an opportunity to celebrate its own culture, background, special interests, and customs while simultaneously sharing them with the wider campus community.

Students especially recommend that groups *co*-sponsor events. Such co-sponsorship has been quite common in recent years. What better way, students ask, to engage classmates from different backgrounds or races or religions in a common pursuit? Even when a speaker, or a topic, is controversial? Students describe working with members of other groups on the planning and implementation of such events as one of the most constructive and enjoyable kinds of learning they have experienced.

One interviewee told us about a group of students interested in the value and effectiveness of bilingual education who decided to organize an evening. They invited four speakers, including two professors who disagreed, the author of the California ballot initiative called "English for the Children," and a member of the California State Assembly who disagreed with that author. These students then assembled a group of organizations to co-sponsor this event. The sponsors included three Latino groups, an Asian-American group, the Harvard-Radcliffe Black Students Association, a Republican Club, and a "Democratic Caucus." A professor from the law school was invited to serve as moderator. The student described the strong impact this evening had on him:

> A lot of us care deeply about bilingual education. I am one of a minority of Latinos here who is strongly opposed. My family came here from Mexico when I was about six, and I know for sure I would never be at Harvard had I become imprisoned in one of those bilingual programs. But I am just one guy. And my opinion is not based on extensive, scholarly study. I do biochemistry here. So it was exciting to participate in this event. I think the most important part of the evening was that we guaranteed a good level of disagreement among the speakers by inviting those four particular people. And getting the different campus groups to co-sponsor it—that served a wonderful purpose.
>
> I am a member of a campus group called Latinas Unidas de Harvard-Radcliffe. Instead of slinking into a corner and just talking among ourselves and always agreeing with ourselves, we got an incredible variety of campus organizations involved. Democrats, Republi-

cans, whites, blacks, Asians, and of course plenty of folks like me. In the process, we got fabulous attendance and real engagement from some people in all these groups. I bet I wasn't the only guy in the room taken aback to see the mix of opinions *within* each of the sponsoring groups about the value of bilingual education in K–12 education. In California, at least, where I come from, I think most non-Latinos assume that Latinos support these programs. I knew this wasn't true, but it took this evening to both affirm what I believed, and, perhaps more important, educate a whole lot of other, non-Latino students about the issues. It was really a grand success.

## CHOOSING AN ATTITUDE

The overall atmosphere on any campus develops as an aggregation of attitudes of the many individuals on that campus. Many students remark on the power of campus leaders, especially student leaders, to set a tone that affects those attitudes. One woman, an Asian-American sophomore, recalls trying to decide, as a new arrival on campus, which of three Asian-American student organizations to join.

At the first introductory meeting of one of these three, I won't name which one, about the only thing the two leaders seemed to offer was a laundry list of grousing. They complained about discrimination against Asian-Americans in admissions, which I found astonishing since we are about 500 percent over-represented relative to our numbers in the United States. Then they complained we didn't have our own, physically more impressive meeting place. Well, by the time this first session ended, they had lost me. Actually, I don't know exactly when it ended, because together with two friends I simply walked out. It was awful. In fact, it was embarrassing.

This young woman says she arrived at this campus full of good will. Good will toward the college. Good will toward other students, faculty, and everyone else. She has strong advice for all new students: make your own judgments. Assume good will on the part of other students, and it will be returned many times over.

More than a few students make similar points about a potential conflict between good will on the part of individuals and the role of campus ethnic and racial and religious organizations. Each of them has developed his or her own way of looking at this potential conflict. For example, one first-year woman told interviewer Shu-Ling Chen: "I get uneasy when people want to separate out into groups instead of thinking about how they might contribute as individuals." Another expressed her worry about group membership by observing to Chen: "I want people to question every single thing I say. People who will say 'no' to me because they think differently. I don't want to go . . . where everyone thinks like me."

Undergraduates report that they think hard about how to retain full individual integrity while participating wholeheartedly in a campus ethnic group. Since most such groups exist, after all, primarily to serve people with similar backgrounds and interests, there is a risk that the individual may be swallowed up in a kind of "groupthink." Fortunately, many students are so aware of this potential problem that they work actively, vigorously, and purposefully to make sure a diversity of ideas is heard even within each student organization.

Most of all, students ask other students to not take being at college for granted. They point out that these few years in college offer a very special opportunity to get to know, and know well, people whom they might never befriend outside the campus atmosphere. It is powerful to hear a Korean-American student from Los Angeles describe her pleasure in living with an African-American roommate from that same city, a city where, according to both these students, race relations between those two groups are not great. It is equally powerful, for similar reasons, to hear about an African-American student from New York City choosing to live with an Orthodox Jew from New York.

The punch line is that students have a choice about what attitude, what point of view, they bring to campus. And undergraduate leaders are in an ideal position to remind their fellow students, especially each year's new arrivals, of the value of taking full advantage of this once-in-a-lifetime opportunity. From my conversations with the students I have had the privilege of interviewing, I am optimistic that the ideal of a "search for common ground" is alive and well among undergraduates. I hope to encourage it on my campus, and I hope that students on many other campuses find this principle congenial as well.

## The Crucial First Few Weeks

Several such small things took place during that same first week, before classes. We all were just getting to know one another. We all were eager to learn about this place, and to make friends. We had a conversation led by my first-year proctor the next evening. She made a similar point about "getting to know people here who are different." And then those essays we got in the mail over the summer kind of set the stage even before arriving here. A lot of small things, cumulatively, during that first week, really set a tone. And I bet that tone, once it is set at the beginning, becomes hard to change.

As I invited undergraduates to make suggestions for how to help diversity work, a certain pattern quickly appeared. Whatever the details of each student's suggestions, they all seem to bunch up, temporally, at the beginning of first year. This would not surprise my colleagues David Pillemer and Sheldon White, who conducted extensive research on how undergraduates and alumni describe and remember critical incidents in their college experience. They discovered exactly the same pattern: memories of critical moments and events cluster heavily in the first few weeks of college. This finding, confirmed by our interviews, has a strong policy implication. The first few weeks of each academic year are a particularly good time for campus leaders to share thoughts and ideas with new students.

An Asian-American senior recalls the impact of one event during orientation week. It was the afternoon of the second day, when several deans offered welcoming remarks to all the new first-year students and their parents. This senior remembers distinctly that one of the deans spoke about the benefits of seeking out and getting to know other first-year students of different backgrounds, ethnic and racial groups, home towns, and substantive interests.

The student says the dean's remarks made a big impression on him. He was devoting 90 percent of his thoughts to academic plans. He was busy moving into his new dorm and getting settled. The dean's words were uplifting yet blunt. And the dean made a specific suggestion, just a few sentences: "Each of you might want to consider, as a personal goal, learning to understand other people. And to understand other people, I have always found it helpful to try to understand how they think. Even better, if it is possible, to understand how they think, I try to understand how they think about themselves. I invite you to reflect on this, as an opportunity."

The student tells this story as representing an important moment in the way he chose to experience college. For him, it set a tone. The tone was particularly strong because he was sitting with the entire first-year class. He knew that all his new classmates, as well as his own parents, were hearing the same remarks. He recalls going back to his room later that afternoon and talking with his three roommates about what the dean "really meant."

This student stresses that now, as a senior, he realizes why that set of remarks from a campus leader mattered a great deal.

> I remember them because those ideas were presented to all of us so soon as new students, with all of us a bit nervous, all eager to do well, all eager to meet new people. Then a group of us actually discussed the dean's remarks over dinner that first week. It was one thing we all had in common—we had all heard the same welcoming presentation. I remember in particular the choice of words, that "boundaries are permeable, and it is worth making the effort to cross them." I know it is a simple enough idea, but coming from a high school where few boundaries were crossed, it seemed important. The main thing is that it set a tone of extending myself to others who are different. I think hitting us right out of the gate, when we first arrived, was critical and a good idea.

This same theme is echoed by many other students. Certain incidents and memories from the first few days and weeks on campus wield a powerful influence on their own behavior. Students learn by living and interacting with others who are different from their old friends and neighbors, and the tone set early on by campus leaders can encourage them to engage in that kind of learning. It is clear that the first few days and weeks on any campus are, for many, a big deal. They set in motion a spirit that some students characterize, several years later, as "something in the air."

## Scheduling Classes Just before Dinner

My faculty colleagues and I talk a lot about student life in our residence halls. We all believe that university life consists of both formal and informal learning. It is obvious that, on any residential campus, students spend a reasonable fraction of their time in their residence hall or dorm. Are there some ways in which we could help students make better use of those hours, ways in which we could enrich those hours substantively?

Student interviewer Anne Clark and I explored this question. Her main finding illustrates yet again the value of gathering ideas and reactions directly from students. Students told us there are indeed ways to strengthen day-to-day life in the residence halls. And what they suggest turns out to be quite different from faculty members' preconceptions about what might work best.

We know that on any residential campus, large or small, if a full-time student spends about 12 hours per week in formal classes, and maybe an additional 3–10 hours in labs or language sessions, that still is under 20 hours per week in formal academic settings. What about the other 148 hours?

So we asked students to suggest how we could capitalize on those other hours, some of which students spend in their dormitories eating, playing, working, socializing, reflecting, or just doing homework.

A big majority of students responded that college is already a high-intensity, high-pressure environment. They reminded us constantly about how many academic responsibilities they already had. Their point was that simply piling on more talks and seminars and formal academic presentations night after night in the dorms is not something most students would applaud. It would be just too much.

But about half of the students made a counter-suggestion. If our college wants to beef up the academic component of residential life, they proposed, how about rescheduling certain classes late in the afternoon, just before dinner? Many were even more specific. Might it be possible, asked dozens of students, to schedule section meetings from large courses so that the sections were held in the dormitories, and the students were assigned to sections by dorm? Since nearly all colleges offer some large courses in which students are divided into sections, this suggestion may apply widely.

The suggestion was in large measure logistical. So let's say a large, popular course called "Justice" or "Shakespeare: The Early Plays" or "Michelangelo" has 200 students. The students suggest that instead of randomly dividing the class into sections of 15–20 for weekly smaller-group discussions, why not create sections by dormitory? Preferably sections that meet in the late afternoon. That way one section will meet from, say, 4:00 to 5:30 P.M. at Dorm X, with all 20 participants being residents of Dorm X. Another section, meeting from 4:00 to 5:30 at Dorm Y, will have 18 students, all from Dorm Y.

What is the big idea here? It's the idea of capitalizing on

meals. Since, on a campus like ours, the residents of each dorm often eat dinner in that dorm, it should be easy for students in each section to go directly from section meeting to dinner as a group. Or even as two or three subgroups. And then, *the substantive conversation from the class section can continue over dinner.* The instructor may or may not join on a given week. But for most students that isn't the important point. The important point is that dinner is an activity everyone in a residence hall routinely partakes of. And by building on students' common experience as classmates in their course section, this scheduling idea offers a simple, straightforward way to encourage a more substantive tone in at least one aspect of dorm life—in this case, one dinner each week for students who choose to attend.

This idea would also work well on campuses where students have their meals at a central dining hall rather than in the dorms. Scheduling classes so they break up at dinnertime would encourage students to walk to the dining hall together and continue their discussions. Furthermore, the idea can be applied to seminars and other classes, not just to sections of large lecture courses.

I am struck by how often students' responses give us, as faculty or administrators, a slightly different idea about how to accomplish a goal. In framing our question about beefing up the quality of dorm life, my colleagues and I had in mind elaborate add-ons—massive additional academic activities in the dorms. It was students who came up with a simple insight that carried the day. They pointed out that they all eat dinner anyway, and that with minor scheduling changes we could make it natural to continue their conversations from their class sections as they moved on to dinner.

After students suggested this straightforward logistical adjustment, we designed a small survey of students who actually met in such course sections in their residence halls. Most of them—82 percent—say they are delighted with this scheduling plan. They are delighted that the sections meet in a seminar room in their dorm. They are delighted that the section discussions can continue over dinner. And, I might add, they are delighted that joining the full group afterward for dinner is optional. Most students don't join every week—about half the time is more typical. The big point is that students have actually changed their behavior. In the direction we hoped. And, like so many other suggestions students make, this positive change was their idea in the first place. Both senior administrators and new arrivals on campus may want to reflect on these suggestions. They come from the experience and wisdom of the students. We're just taking notes.

## Getting in Students' Way

At the beginning of this book, I quoted a dean from another university who said the strategy at his college was to admit a talented group of students and then just "get out of their way." It seems clear to me from the dozens of anecdotes and examples in this book that campus leaders should indeed implement the first part of that plan—admit a talented group of students—and then do exactly the opposite of that dean's recommendation. They should make a thoughtful, evidence-based, purposeful effort to get *in* each student's way. In fact, shaping a certain kind of campus culture may be the biggest contribution campus leaders can make.

In our interviews, student after student has shared stories that cumulatively illustrate an overarching theme, and I want to stress it. That theme is the interplay, the complex interaction, among different parts of campus life. Learning in classes can be enhanced, sometimes dramatically, by activities outside of classes. Good advice on course selection can make the difference between a happy young scholar and a frustrated one. Students report that their most powerful memories come from incidents and experiences outside of classes, usually during interactions with fellow students. These experiences are heavily influenced by residential living choices, which in turn are influenced by campus policies concerning who gets to live where.

This key idea shines through many student anecdotes: life at college is a complex system, with interrelated parts. Choosing which classes to take when, figuring out how to get to know professors, relating activities outside of classes to learning in formal courses, and especially decisions about whom to live with at a time of dramatically changing demographics on campus—these are choices each student must make.

So a critical role for campus leaders is to "get in the way" of each student, to help that young adult evaluate and re-evaluate his or her choices, always in the spirit of trying to do just a bit better next time. After ten years of research, we now have a substantial number of specific suggestions we can make to undergraduates. Students can and should do many things on their own. Yet adults, as campus leaders, should not hesitate to help.

I want to close with my favorite anecdote. It is so rich that I find it hard to tell whether it is politically tilted to the left or to the right—and perhaps that's why I find it so appealing. I asked a graduating senior whether he could go beyond platitudes about the changing demographics on campus and give a specific example of the complexity of modern campus life that he actually experienced. I also asked if he

could offer future students any lessons from his experience.
Here is his response:

You ask whether diversity had any impact on my learning here at college. In some ways it has been the single
biggest factor that affected my experience here. I am
very happy in Cabot House as a senior. Looking back,
much of it started because of sophomore tutorial. Seven
of us at Cabot House are doing social studies. The department organized sophomore tutorial so that the
seven of us met every week right at the House. The instructor was a young economist. He played an important role in unexpected ways.

First let me tell you about the seven of us. There were
two white guys, two white women, a man from India, a
black woman, and a Chinese-American man. We didn't
all know each other yet, since we had just arrived at the
House. This was our first course meeting. Everything
was new. I think when everyone looked at the reading
list we all felt pretty overwhelmed. Reading unending
amounts of material from Weber, Durkheim, Burke,
Adam Smith, Karl Marx, John Stuart Mill, Freud, and
some other political philosophers had us all a little
nervous.

Now here is where the diversity among the group
began to matter. One of the women said she couldn't
help noticing there was not exactly a heavy representa-
tion of people like her on the reading list. The black
woman agreed. The instructor seemed hesitant to give a
speech about why this was a great reading list, which in
my eyes it was. Then the other white woman said
something like, yes the reading list consisted of a dozen

dead white males. But they are the "great" political philosophers and so let's not argue about the reading list. What she would like to do, she suggested, is take a more current political controversy, and after the group has discussed each author's work, let's try to apply that author's ideas to the current controversy.

So the Asian guy suggested we take affirmative action as the current controversy. There was total silence for a moment. We all looked around the table to see everyone's reaction. Then our instructor spoke up. He said he thought the idea sounded great, as long as we didn't give short shrift to those reading assignments. He assured us some of those readings were hard going. Since it was our first session and there was no assignment for that day, we took a few minutes to share our views about affirmative action. No one was shy, and there was plenty of disagreement. To oversimplify a little, two of the whites were for affirmative action, and two, including me, were against. The Indian guy was against, the black woman was for, and the Asian guy was against. And of course there were shadings of these opinions. A lot of those differences were obviously shaped by the ethnic diversity in the room, and the different backgrounds we had growing up.

Well, that whole year's tutorial made my Harvard education. First, we were very respectful of one another's views, because we all understood those views had evolved from our very different backgrounds. After all, I have to be pretty tactful as a white guy when I tell a talented black woman I think she is hurting herself in the long run by supporting affirmative action. Some of this stuff can be pretty personal. Second, we had great discussions nearly every week, because none of us could possibly ever really know what Freud or Durkheim or Weber would have thought of affirmative action. And our instructor pushed us really hard to relate our arguments to each week's readings, so the discussions never became some sort of touchy-feely waste of time. If anything, our discussions helped to clarify the readings.

Your original question was about the educational effects of diversity. Well, the effects were strong. And lasting. Everyone read the assigned authors carefully. Partly because some are not so easy to understand. But partly because we knew we would be discussing how those writings would relate to modern debates about affirmative action. You think that is easy? It's not. Then, sometimes people got to bring their personal backgrounds into the conversation.

One time the Asian guy turned to the black woman who supports affirmative action and basically said, "I arrived here in America when I was six years old, and my parents had nothing. We were penniless refugees. You grew up in Scarsdale. How can you argue for affirmative action after reading John Stuart Mill and Edmund Burke? And if affirmative action exists, why are you a candidate for it? And when does it end? Your parents are well off. They are highly educated. You went to a great high school. You are now at Harvard. When you graduate, do you expect on top of all that to still get preferences in hiring? When should affirmative action end for you?"

I particularly remember that day because it was an electric moment. It was the first time I could see how our conversations were leading people around the table to change their minds. That day was also a test of our civility to one another, and our capacity to disagree with respect. We all passed that test with flying colors. No one was offended by these conversations. We all treated them as a special opportunity to discuss a topic that is sometimes awkward, and even to use that topic as a wedge to help all of us understand the writings of those very distinguished dead white males, whom I happen to admire.

Now as a senior I can say that whole year was the best experience I had here. Five of the seven of us have remained close friends for three years. We all are still at Cabot House. And the difference between these friends and all my other friends is that a significant part of our friendship is based around substantive discussions about ideas. None of us feels hesitant about initiating a discussion or question about Freud or whomever. After all, we did it every week for a whole year together in a room here where we live, right down the hall. And we certainly learned a lot about each other, and from each other.

Mixing our different personal backgrounds, that came from growing up in different circumstances, with some back-breakingly dense readings was a new experience for me. For example, it made me rethink what a meritocracy really means. I hadn't thought of it before as so complicated. Now I do. I actually changed my mind about how a meritocracy might work because of these discussions. And I saw other students in the group gradually change their minds, or temper their views. Watching those changes was amazing. Isn't that what a college education is all about? And now, to answer your original question about the educational impact of diversity, can you ever imagine seven white guys, all just like me, sitting around a table and accomplishing the same thing?

THE ASSESSMENT PROJECT

REFERENCES

ACKNOWLEDGMENTS

INDEX

# THE ASSESSMENT PROJECT

In 1986 the president of Harvard University, Derek Bok, invited me to assemble a group of colleagues to start a long-term program of research and assessment to evaluate the effectiveness of what the university does, and to devise ways to improve it. How well do we teach now, and what changes will make it better? How well do we advise students now, and what changes will make it better? Do our students write enough? How do we know? Can we improve this? Do we demand enough of our students? Do our faculty members help students to become more effective students? How can we do this even better?

Since the seminars began at Harvard, much of the work inevitably has been done at Harvard. But although we adopted the name "Harvard Assessment Seminars," many colleagues from other colleges and universities have been involved from the outset. We began as a group of sixty-five people representing twenty-five different colleges and universities.

Our group immediately decided to view assessment in a particular way. For some people the word "assessment" might connote a focus on asking "How much do students know?"—but that was not what we wanted to emphasize. It is an interesting question, but our goal was different. Our goal was and is to explore innovation in teaching, in curriculum, and in advising. We work to understand the effectiveness of each innovation. A key question we examine is

217

under what conditions students learn best, both inside and outside of classrooms. We believe that slow but steady improvement in instruction and advising can make college ever more effective.

We also quickly and unanimously agreed that our explorations *must all be first-class science.* Without good science, we would accomplish nothing. The students we interview expect care and rigor. They are contributing their precious time. It would be unforgivable to waste this time. We never forget that principle.

Furthermore, we agreed that each project must be designed to gather information *in a form that would help to guide educational policy decisions.* Every time a project is proposed, I ask the same question: "How will this project help professors, advisors, staff members, or students to do their work better?"

To illustrate this emphasis on policy, consider two possible investigations connected to students' writing. The first might focus on the question, "How well do our students write?" A useful question. But how will answering it help a writing teacher, or a student, do a better job in the future? Taken alone, such a project will generate information. It may stimulate discussion. But how will knowing that "on the average our undergraduates write pretty well" lead to improvements in policy? What will change on campus as a result of this finding?

Contrast this with an effort designed to inform policy change. At any college, some entering freshmen write better than others. Teachers must deal with these differences. The goal of an assessment project with an emphasis on policy is to come up with helpful advice for faculty and students. For example, focus on the weaker writers. Follow them throughout a freshman writing course. Some get a C-minus on their first essay but end the year with A-minus essays. Others begin with C-minus essays and end with C-minus essays. Faculty members on any campus can ask: "Why do some students improve their writing dramatically in their first year here, while others hardly improve at all? What factors in teaching, and in how students work on writing outside of class, distinguish between students who improve dramatically and those who don't?" Notice that this policy-oriented formulation changes the emphasis of the investigation toward findings that can lead to *action*. We constantly focus on the real-world policy implications of each project. We all want to avoid a situation in which researchers present findings about strengthening college only to other researchers, with no impact on teaching, curriculum, or college life.

Our mode of working engages both faculty members and students. We work together closely. In retrospect, this is probably the single most important decision that shapes successful projects. Faculty members do the main work of exploring innovations in curriculum and teaching and then trying them out. And the many students who participate offer two crucial boosts. First, they help to shape instruments for interviewing other students, and after careful training they do interviews. Second, under faculty supervision, they do much of the nitty-gritty synthesis and analysis of data. To date, several undergraduate honors theses and six doctoral dissertations have grown out of this work.

Neil Rudenstine, who succeeded Bok as president of Harvard in 1991, has overseen changes in the way we do our work, as well as in the projects we focus on. The major change is that after several years of meeting monthly as a group of sixty-five people, we had generated so many good ideas that we decided we should concentrate on getting the work done. So each project now moves forward on a smaller scale. When a group of faculty members identifies a topic, the faculty work with carefully trained and supervised student interviewers, who gather information from their fellow undergraduates to carry out the project.

When President Rudenstine took office, he identified three priorities that he urged our group to explore. First, what is the educational impact on students of the increasing diversity of those who attend Harvard? And how can the college encourage students to learn, both in classes and in interactions outside of classes, from this new diversity? Second, since undergraduates at Harvard, as at many other residential colleges, spend much of their time in their dorms or residence halls, what initiatives or programs might enhance this part of their lives? Third, how important is class size for students' learning, engagement with their academic work, and overall academic experience? This book presents our findings to date on these topics.

Of course, answers to the three questions are not static. For example, the exponential growth of technology, and the new ways of using it for instruction, may well change the value of very small classes, tutorials, and seminars in ways we cannot yet predict. Nonetheless, I share this background about the origins of all our work to help readers set our findings in a context. Ideas for projects reported in this book have come from students, from faculty, and from university presidents.

## Advantages of Interviews

A key methodological decision we made at the beginning was to gather information from in-depth interviews. I would like to illustrate the value of focusing on results from interview data. Suppose undergraduates at a college are asked a question about race relations on campus. In a check-box, coded questionnaire format, each might be invited to check one of five alternatives:

0 = Race relations are terrible.
1 = Race relations are poor.
2 = Race relations are neutral.
3 = Race relations are good.
4 = Race relations are excellent.

If two-thirds of all students choose "good," one-third choose "excellent," and no one chooses anything else, the overall numerical average is 3.33. According to most colleges' grade-point format, this is exactly a B+. So imagine the headline in the local newspaper: "Students Rate Campus Race Relations as B+." And indeed that is numerically correct. Yet such a finding conveys the sense that relations are not especially good.

In contrast, suppose those same findings are reported simply and concisely in words:

No undergraduates say race relations are terrible.
No undergraduates say race relations are poor.
No undergraduates say race relations are neutral.
Two-thirds of all undergraduates say race relations are good.
One-third of all undergraduates say race relations are excellent.

Here a noticeably different picture emerges. It has a different tone, and it invites a different interpretation. It illustrates the value of reporting more detailed findings rather than just a summary statistic. It is a special pleasure for me, as a professional statistician, to find circumstances in which detailed verbal summaries yield clearer interpretations than summary indexes.

My faculty colleagues are big fans of something called "face validity." So the findings reported in this book capitalize on this idea. Specifically, take the topic of what constitutes effective course design. Are there certain courses in which students report that they learn especially much and become especially engaged? If one interviewer asked this question of, say, 240 undergraduates, and came up with several features of especially effective courses, we would all be delighted to hear such a finding. My colleagues and I might even try to build as many of these positive features as possible into our own teaching.

Now suppose six different interviewers, say a professor and five students, after careful planning and training, interview forty undergraduates each. Working independently, they ask the same questions about especially effective courses. If all six interviewers separately summarize their findings and the summaries are consistent, then these findings have strong "face validity." Chances are that if six different interviewers, including both faculty and students, all find the same thing, then that thing is probably roughly right. This is the big advantage of using multiple interviewers. The findings presented in this book do not come from any one person's idiosyncratic perspective.

## What I Have Learned

Organizing and directing the research reported in this book has taught me lessons about both the opportunities and the pitfalls of such a venture. The work has not been without some controversy. I assume other colleges and universities may undergo similar experiences. Here I would like to share seven lessons I have learned about assessment.

## FACULTY INITIATIVE IS IMPORTANT

Faculty members must assume a central role in directing assessment projects and policy-oriented innovations to improve teaching, advising, and student life. As I invited faculty from twenty-five colleges to participate in the Harvard Assessment Seminars, the questions I was asked most often were, "Is this a faculty initiative? Will faculty shape the investigations?"

I was a bit taken aback by these questions. I had assumed that of course the answer would be yes. But gradually I learned that many faculty members were concerned they might become little more than research assistants for someone else. Most faculty are busy, and most of the work of their professional life has little to do with assessment. If they can't help to shape the important questions and can't initiate projects to help their teaching, they may not participate at all.

## CLARIFY WHAT ASSESSMENT MEANS

Research on college effectiveness, and especially the word "assessment," means different things to different people. For example, faculty perspectives are somewhat different at public and private universities. An increasing number of state legislatures are requiring specific procedures and steps for colleges to conduct self-evaluations. Some public institutions feel under the gun to administer large-scale standardized tests to assess "what students know now."

But this is not the type of question that sparks excitement at private colleges, at least those represented in our assessment seminars. Rather than defining assessment as testing what students know now, my colleagues define it as a process of evaluating and improving current programs, encouraging innovations, and then evaluating each innovation's effectiveness. The key step is systematic gathering of information for sustained improvement. And always with an eye toward helping faculty or students work more effectively.

Faculty members bring diverse ideas and suggestions to such an enterprise. Our group quickly agreed that it is crucial to encourage and assess innovations both inside and outside the classroom. Many faculty members are eager to improve classroom teaching, so they are especially interested in trying in-class innovations. Some are exploring ways to improve teaching effectiveness without introducing elaborate new equipment. Others are eager to use new technology, yet want to see compelling evidence that such equipment can improve students' learning. A third group feels the biggest gains in student performance will come from a sustained effort to improve academic advising, rather than from changes in classroom teaching.

It is crucial to accommodate these different views. They lead to projects that turn up useful results. For example, it was suggestions from academic advisors that led to the in-class experiments that got students working in small groups. And many fans of high-tech equipment are surprised to learn how effective some low-tech classroom teaching innovations can be. These include, for example, the one-minute paper and videotaping students in small groups and then having an experienced debriefer watch the tape with each student.

## INVOLVE STUDENTS IN THE RESEARCH

At first, I did not invite any students to participate in the assessment seminars. Since most faculty participants spend much of every day teaching and working with students, I assumed they would prefer to spend this extra time working only with colleagues. Bad mistake. I couldn't have been more wrong. All of our work—its planning, its execution, and even the establishing of the importance of different possible research efforts—has been enriched enormously by student participation.

Students took great initiative. Though none were invited at first, I soon began to receive calls. These calls continue. Some are from graduate students interested in higher education as a substantive field. Others are from specialists in statistics and research design. Still others are from undergraduates who want to do their honors theses on topics connected to understanding and strengthening their environment at college. I finally realized that many students have a genuine interest in policy research on colleges. And they are eager to do the nitty-gritty work on projects—interviewing, data collection, and computer analyses.

The faculty, in turn, are able to offer these students two incentives. One is modest financial support. Most students need it and all appreciate it. The other incentive, far more important in the long run, is intense and careful faculty supervision. For example, ten graduate students volunteered to carry out in-depth interviews with Harvard sophomores. Their goal was to probe why some students flourish in their first year here while others, with similar SAT scores and high school grades, are less successful. Professor David Riesman invited these ten students, together with several faculty members, to his home for two evenings of training. The agenda was to learn how to interview undergraduates in a reliable and productive way. Several of the student interviewers told me later that the two evenings at Professor Riesman's home, working with senior faculty, were not only useful, they were the two most memorable evenings of their Harvard years.

## SENIOR ADMINISTRATIVE SUPPORT IS HELPFUL

For our research, President Bok provided support in two ways. First, he advocated on-campus research and assessment in his annual report of 1986, thus publicly giving this work a high priority. As a result, busy faculty and administrators understood that by participating in assessment they could shape policy decisions in the future.

Second, Bok made a clear statement by allocating seed money to the seminars. This support got our seminars started, funded student assistants, and created a series of dinners for our participants. It is clear in retrospect that this funding emphasized high administrative priority from the president's office from the outset.

President Rudenstine continues this strong statement by supporting both the work on examining diversity and a longitudinal study of how students improve their writing at college. The point here is straightforward. Support from the president, especially financial support, conveys a strong message to the entire college community about the importance of this work.

## AIM FOR REAL POLICY CHANGE

A crucial agenda item at our earliest meetings was "to identify the biggest risk we face so as to reduce the chance of failure." We quickly recognized the risk that assessment projects may become merely theoretical investigations conducted by people disconnected from policy decisions, who then report their findings only to similar research specialists. To reduce this risk, each project team is now encouraged to ask itself repeatedly, "What are the policy implications of our work? How can our findings improve teaching (or curricula, or advising, or student services)?"

Other campuses can benefit from our experience. It is critical to emphasize gathering information that will actually improve education. In the end, the test of the value of any piece of work is whether or not it helps to coordinate the work of faculty, administrators, and students to shape real change. If on-campus evaluation is undertaken simply to create another academic publication, it will serve a limited purpose.

## PLAN TO DISSEMINATE SUCCESSFUL INNOVATIONS

Research about teaching and learning and the educational impact of diversity must gain enough public notice on campus so that positive findings can be adopted widely. An example from our early meetings illustrates this. Many faculty were present at a session focusing on effective teaching innovations. One particularly simple innovation—the one-minute paper—was found to yield large benefits to both students and faculty. Several faculty members who attended subsequently discussed this finding with their colleagues in their own departments. Because many on the faculty know about our on-campus research, and know that one of its purposes is to encourage helpful tools for teaching, a receptive audience was waiting.

## ENCOURAGE INNOVATION AND EVALUATION

What does a dean or department chairman typically do, if each of five faculty members comes, individually, to propose a new and better way to teach biology? Most deans on most campuses will say "good luck" to each of them, and they will mean it. Then, after the five professors have tried out their innovations in the classroom, those who succeed in improving biology instruction will be rewarded either privately or publicly.

A critical message from our work is that such administrative action doesn't do much to encourage steady and widespread improvement. If five faculty members propose new and different ways to teach biology, administrators may think there is little chance all five will succeed in doing it better than the old way. Indeed, the administrators are likely to be delighted if just one of these faculty members really does it significantly better than the old way. We all learn to treasure any improvement. After all, developing new ways to teach that are demonstrably better than existing practice is not easy. Many people have thought for many years about how to teach effectively. It would be astonishing if every new idea worked well.

Might it make good sense, then, to stimulate, encourage, and even reward all five faculty members who want to innovate? And to emphasize to each of them the key step of putting into place a serious, scientifically valid effort to assess each new method's effectiveness? This would communicate that the campus honors the process of innovation and also the process of systematic evaluation. Most important, we should not be dismayed if any particular innovation does not turn out to be a grand success. By encouraging both innovation and systematic assessment, any campus embarks on a longer-term program of steady improvement. Such a program will inevitably include both successes and failures.

Creating such an environment can be a challenge. It is natural for most faculty members, and I include myself, to highlight new courses or teaching methods only when they work well. It is a wonderful feeling to succeed. But evidence from Harvard tells us it is possible to create a climate that rewards innovation and assessment *as a process.* This process will identify failures as well as successes. Faculty members and administrators must agree to accept this possibility of two steps forward and one step back. It can lead to a remarkable upsurge in efforts to improve education for all students.

# REFERENCES

Angelo, T. A. Assessing what matters: How participation in work, athletics and extracurriculars relates to the academic success and personal satisfaction of Harvard undergraduates. A first report on the Harvard Assessment Seminars' 1988 interview study. 1989.

Bok, D. C. The president's report: 1984–1985. February 1986. Available from the Office of the President, Harvard University, Massachusetts Hall, Cambridge, MA 02138.

Buchanan, C. H., G. Feletti, C. Krupnick, G. Lowery, J. McLaughlin, D. Riesman, B. Snyder, and J. Wu. The impact of Harvard College on freshman learning. A pilot study conducted in the Harvard Seminar on Assessment, 1990.

Bushey, B. The Moral Reasoning 30 sectioning experiment. Presented at the Harvard Assessment Seminars, April 10, 1989. Available from the Harvard Assessment Seminars, Graduate School of Education, Cambridge, MA 02138.

——. Writing improvement in the Harvard Expository Writing Program: Policy recommendations, suggestions for faculty, and suggestions for students. Policy report presented to President Bok, May 1991, on behalf of the Harvard Assessment Seminars.

——. What helps weak writers learn to write better: A pilot study in the Harvard Expository Writing Program. Doctoral dissertation, Harvard Graduate School of Education, 1991.

Carmichael, D. Diversity and the analytical toolbox: Learning to take advantage of our differences. Policy analysis exercise, Kennedy School of Government, Harvard University, April 14, 1993.

Chen, Shu-Ling. First-year students' opinions of ethnic diversity at

Harvard. Completed for the Harvard Assessment Seminars Diversity Project, July 1996.

Civian, J. Summary of student responses regarding foreign languages. Prepared for the Harvard Assessment Seminars, July 1989.

Clark, A. R. Examining Harvard/Radcliffe undergraduate tutorials: A pilot study. Enhancing the success of tutorials: Suggestions for tutors and for students. Prepared for the Harvard Assessment Seminars, Fall 1992.

——. House academic life: Impressions and suggestions from seventy-seven undergraduates. Prepared for the Harvard Assessment Seminars, 1993.

Committee on Undergraduate Education. Course evaluation guide. Frederick S. Chung, editor-in-chief. Produced by Harvard College undergraduates under guidelines set by the Committee on Undergraduate Education, 1990–1991.

Dushay, J. Women, men, and the natural sciences and math at Harvard/Radcliffe. A pilot study. Paper for Seminar on Assessment, May 1991.

Eisenmann, A. M. Assessing personal satisfaction and academic success in the freshman year at Harvard/Radcliffe: A look at academic experiences, faculty/student interaction, and advising. Harvard Assessment Seminars, May 1989. Available from Office of the Dean for Student Affairs, 84 Massachusetts Avenue, Massachusetts Institute of Technology, Cambridge, MA 02139.

Eng, R. Asian-American students: Confucianism and morality. Qualifying paper submitted to the Harvard Graduate School of Education, December 1992.

——. Road to virtue: The moral world of Chinese and Korean-American students. Doctoral dissertation, Harvard Graduate School of Education, 1994.

Fadiman, Anne. Procrustes and the culture wars. Phi Beta Kappa oration delivered June 3, 1997, Harvard University.

Fincke, A. J. The impact of diversity on the experience of Harvard undergraduates: A report of findings from 50 in-depth, one-to-one interviews. Completed for the Harvard Assessment Seminars Diversity Project, 1997–1998.

Fulkerson, F. E., and G. Martin. Effects of exam frequency on student performance, evaluations of instructors, and test anxiety. *Teaching of Psychology* 8 (1981): 90–93.

Gates, Henry Louis, Jr. The ethics of identity. Essay sent to incoming students, Harvard College, summer 2000.

Gilbert, J. P., R. J. Light, and F. Mosteller. Assessing social innovation: an empirical base for policy. In C. A. Bennett and A. A. Lumsdaine, eds., *Evaluation and Experiment* (New York: Academic Press, 1975).

Goldhaber, S. The impact of religious diversity on student experiences: Findings from 40 one-on-one interviews with observant Catholic, Protestant, Jewish, and Muslim Harvard undergraduates. Completed for the Harvard Assessment Seminars Diversity Project, 1997–1998.

Hokanson, K. Preliminary results of satisfaction ratings: Comparison of alumni and undergraduate responses. Presented to the Harvard Assessment Seminars, April 10, 1989. Available from the Harvard Assessment Seminars, Graduate School of Education, Cambridge, MA 02138.

———. Preliminary results from the foreign language section of the young alumni survey. Presented to the Harvard Assessment Seminars, April 10, 1989.

Homer, M. The Mellon Program for mentored research grants: An evaluation. Harvard Office of Student Employment, 1992.

Homer, M., and N. Kim. The Ford Program for undergraduate research: A survey of 1988 and 1989 Ford Grant recipients. Harvard Office of Student Employment, 1993.

Klein, M. Problem sets in introductory math and science classes at Harvard College: Observations, policy recommendations, and suggestions for faculty and students. Prepared for the Harvard Assessment Seminars, 1992.

Korn, L. M. Harvard students' strategies of self-presentation: minimizing the impression of academic competence for a peer audience. Undergraduate honors thesis, Department of Psychology, Harvard University, April 1993.

Lewis, D. M. A study of persistence in the sciences. Doctoral dissertation, Harvard Graduate School of Education, 1994.

Light, K. W. Analyzing freshman time-use to improve freshman advising at Harvard. Doctoral dissertation, Harvard Graduate School of Education, 1991.

Light, R. J. The Harvard Assessment Seminars: First report. Explorations with students and faculty about teaching, learning, and student life. 1990.

——. The Harvard Assessment Seminars: Second report. Explorations with students and faculty about teaching, learning, and student life. 1992.

Light, R. J., J. D. Singer, and J. B. Willett. *By Design: Planning Research on Higher Education.* Cambridge, MA: Harvard University Press, 1990.

Magnani, C. The Radcliffe Research Partnership Program: An evaluation of its effectiveness in mentoring women students. Report prepared for the Dean of Radcliffe College and the Harvard Assessment Seminars, 1992.

Merrow, S. Reflections on academic mentoring and partnership relationships: An evaluative study of the 1993–1994 Radcliffe Research Partnership Program. Prepared for the Harvard Assessment Seminars, May 1994.

Middleton, M. Adjusting expectations during the freshman year: A survey of Harvard and Radcliffe freshmen with suggestions for their instructors. 1993.

Mosteller, F. The muddiest point in the lecture as a feedback device. *On Teaching and Learning* 3 (April 1989): 10–21.

Nguyen, Thanh. A evaluation of the Radcliffe Research Partners Program. Prepared for the Dean of Radcliffe College and the Harvard Assessment Seminars, 1994.

Pillemer, D. B., L. R. Goldsmith, A. T. Panter, and S. H. White. Very long-term memories of the first year in college. *Journal of Experimental Psychology: Learning, Memory and Cognition* 14 (1988): 709–715.

Pillemer, D. B., E. Rhinehart, and S. H. White. Memories of life transitions: The first year in college. *Human Learning* 5 (1986): 109–123.

Sachs, J. The role of arts activities in Harvard undergraduates' lives. Prepared for the Harvard Assessment Seminars, 1994.

Shlipak, A. M. Engineering and physics as cultural systems: Impressions of science students at Harvard/Radcliffe. Undergraduate honors thesis, Department of Anthropology, Harvard University, 1988.

Sommers, N. A study of undergraduate writing at Harvard. Prepared by the director of the Harvard Expository Writing Program, 1994.

Steinglass, E. E. The multiple roles of teaching fellows in undergraduate writing. Prepared for the Expository Writing Program, 1993.

Ware, N., N. Steckler, and J. Leserman. Undergraduate women: Who chooses a science major? *Journal of Higher Education* 56 (January/February 1985): 73–84.

Weiss, L. The effects of part-time work and intercollegiate athletics on students' perceptions of their experiences at Harvard College: Recommendations for policy. Undergraduate honors thesis, Department of Sociology, Harvard University, 1988.

———. High-impact experiences and Harvard College undergraduates. A study supported by the Harvard Seminar on Assessment, January 1988.

Wilson, R. C. Improving faculty teaching: Effective use of student evaluations and consultants. *Journal of Higher Education* 57 (March/April 1986): 196–211.

Worth, R. Relationships among admissions credentials, the college experience, and postgraduate outcomes: A survey of the Harvard/Radcliffe classes of 1977. Doctoral dissertation, Harvard Graduate School of Education, 1990.

# ACKNOWLEDGMENTS

This book is different from any other task I have ever undertaken. Ultimately, it exists because of unwavering support from two Harvard Presidents, Derek Bok and Neil Rudenstine. Each suggested certain key ideas that animate this book.

Many of the projects I describe in these chapters were suggested by colleagues from more than two dozen colleges and universities. I am grateful to them. Students played a critical role in gathering data, conducting interviews, and analyzing findings. This book is truly a synthesis of work done by dozens of people, especially students.

I especially want to acknowledge the contributions of the three dozen extraordinary student interviewers. They interviewed their fellow students, contributed hypotheses, brought talent, patience, and passion to the venture, and helped with data analysis. Our projects simply couldn't have been done without them. I have cited their contributions throughout the text and in the References.

Thomas Angelo played a key role in getting our first projects organized. Tom served as assistant director of our enterprise, and it was his initiative that generated our first set of findings.

A special pleasure of working closely with my editor at Harvard University Press, Elizabeth Knoll, was that she pushed me just hard enough to capitalize on my enthusiasm, yet never for a moment gave way on her unrelenting insistence for both rigor and clarity. I am privileged that she devoted much time and energy to this project.

My manuscript editor at the Press, Camille Smith, played a special role. To say her changes improved the book significantly doesn't capture the full richness of her contributions. Camille has edited all three books I have written for Harvard Press. Any author who works with her is fortunate.

I also thank Michael Aronson, whose pursuit of this manuscript for Harvard University Press spanned several years. His good-spirited perseverance was always helpful, and I appreciate it.

Laura Medeiros, my staff assistant, helped with all aspects of preparing the manuscript and was my regular computer consultant. Yet her biggest contribution was her superb judgment. She served as a sounding board for choosing particular anecdotes to include. Her suggestions helped me to improve the manuscript.

At Harvard College, several deans over twelve years encouraged me to explore a broad range of questions. Their willingness to examine areas for improvement as well as our college's areas of obvious strength is courageous. These deans include Jeremy Knowles, Harry Lewis, Elizabeth Studley Nathans, William Fitzsimmons, and, most especially, Archie Epps.

Substantial financial assistance from the Andrew W. Mellon Foundation, a second foundation that chooses to remain anonymous, and the President's Discretionary Fund at Harvard was critical throughout nearly fifteen years of research. The Mellon Foundation, in particular, awarded two long-term grants that facilitate the sustained effort required by this project. I thank these generous people and organizations. All royalties from this book will be donated to undergraduate scholarships.

# INDEX

Wilson, Robert, 69

Women, books recommended by, 152–153

Work: volunteer, 18–20, 28–30; paid, 27–28, 30

Workloads, in science courses, 72–74

Worth, Robin, 54

Writing, 10, 54–55; student engagement in, 55–56; structure of assignments, 56–57; amount of, 57–58; improvement of, 58–65; for fellow students, 63–65; one-minute papers, 66–69